Teaching Scuba Diving

Teaching Scuba Diving

BS AC

The British Sub-Aqua Club

EBURY PRESS

London

First published in 1996

3 5 7 9 10 8 6 4 2

First published in the United Kingdom in 1996 by Ebury Press
Random House, 20 Vauxhall Bridge Road, London SW1V 2SA

Random House Australia (Pty) Limited
20 Alfred Street, Milsons Point, Sydney,
New South Wales 2061, Australia

Random House New Zealand Limited
187 Poland Road, Glenfield, Auckland 10, New Zealand

Random House South Africa (Pty) Limited
PO Box 337, Bergvlei, South Africa

Random House UK Limited Reg. No. 954009

A CIP catalogue record for this book is available from the British Library

ISBN 0 09 174008 8

Printed and bound in Great Britain by Scotprint, Haddington

Contents

Foreword

Along with thousands of other individuals, learning to dive and exploring the underwater world, the last true frontier on earth, has had a profound impact upon my life. However many excursions beneath the waves I make, the sheer joy of just being there continues to invigorate and inspire me.

Learning to dive safely was the result of someone having the knowledge, skill, experience and patience to teach me. When I became more experienced, I wanted to pass on my diving skills to others. It was only when I became a scuba instructor that I discovered the responsibilities, challenges, rewards, and pleasures that introducing someone else to the underwater world can bring.

The British Sub-Aqua Club is the worlds' largest diving club with over 40 years history, its instructors have trained many thousands of safe and capable divers. The BSAC's success in diver training has, in the main, been as a result of an extremely well developed programme for educating, developing, examining and certifying instructors. Today this programme continues to be held in worldwide regard and has often been emulated, but never bettered. All the contributors to this manual are both very experienced divers and highly talented instructors. *Teaching Scuba Diving* is a distillation of all their years of experience at teaching diving.

Clearly no book can substitute for practical experience, but within these pages are the foundations upon which you can build, to become a knowledgeable and proficient scuba diving instructor. It is also an invaluable reference tool for those already qualified as instructors.

The 'core skills' needed by scuba divers are the same the world over, similarly the basic skills and attributes required by the scuba diving instructor are not dependent upon the training agency they represent. If you aspire to be, or are already, a scuba diving instructor you should read this manual.

I wish you well in your diving and instruction.

Bob Boler
BSAC National Diving Officer

Acknowledgements

The British Sub-Aqua Club gratefully acknowledges the efforts of the following persons who have contributed to this publication:

Editors:
Mike Busuttili
Mike Holbrook

Contributors:
Bob Boler
Mike Busuttili
Trevor Davies
Deric Ellerby
Jerry Hazzard
Mike Holbrook
Howard Painter
Mike Todd

The Scuba Instructor

The Scuba Instructor

As air breathing creatures we are well removed from our natural environment when underwater swimming. In order to survive, let alone enjoy such activities we must acquire a range of skills and knowledge that are not part of our normal experience. This is most satisfactorily provided by a qualified scuba instructor. An instructor is someone who teaches, informs and directs. Applying this definition to the diving situation we can start to understand what is needed of a scuba instructor.

Firstly it is essential for any instructor to have high personal skill levels and an extensive knowledge in the subject they are going to instruct. Inevitably this will demand an appropriate base of practical experience. Additional teaching skills such as demonstrating, tutoring, communicating and supervising must then be added to these diving skills to produce an effective instructor.

People who are taught by a good instructor will learn good diving practices from the start, whereas uncorrected bad habits learnt during early training are very difficult to rectify later. Many accidents can be traced back to such habits, which in turn are the result of poor or inadequate instruction.

Motivation

To be able to teach people a sport that you enjoy, and wish to share with them, is probably the most rewarding and stimulating of reasons to become a scuba instructor. Because of increased leisure time, peoples' participation in all forms of sporting activity has grown and will continue to grow for the foreseeable future.

Scuba diving continues to be a popular adventure sport and is enjoyed by more and more people every year. The popularity of scuba diving, particularly as a holiday activity, has also provided opportunities for instructors to teach professionally either as an employee in a dive resort centre or school, others by investing in their own scuba training facility.

The term 'professional instructor' is usually associated with those who derive their living from teaching scuba. However, it is important to understand that there are also 'professional' amateurs who teach for no reward other than the satisfaction gained from teaching others a sport they enjoy. Within The British Sub-Aqua Club the majority of scuba training is conducted by such qualified amateur instructors.

Whether paid or unpaid, scuba instruction requires the same degree of professional expertise. Instruction is an activity which needs to be mastered in the same way as any other pursuit. It comprises of skills which must be gained and knowledge which must be absorbed, if the teaching precess is to be successful. There is a well known dictum that the best way to learn anything is to teach it! Certainly becoming an effective scuba instructor is guaranteed to improve and develop your own diving skills and experience, which will benefit you as well as your students.

Qualities and personal skills

There are a number of important qualities and personal skills that all instructors, particularly scuba instructors, should have, or acquire. In this respect, skills can be categorized as items which can be learnt, while qualities can be thought of as desirable personal traits to be polished and developed. It is obvious that to be credible as a scuba instructor you must have complete personal mastery of all the basic practical exercises that make up underwater swimming.

The standards you apply to your own performance in such activities as kitting up, mask clearing, finning and buoyancy control must be of the highest. Equally your knowledge of diving and diving theory must be both deeper and broader than that needed by your students. If your stature as a teacher of scuba is going to be convincing, you must be able to satisfy all reasonable enquiries from your students.

All of this must be based on a wide experience gained from many different diving activities, conditions and situations, inevitably accumulated over an appropriate period of time. Successfully absorbing the lessons of such experience will provide you with the necessary confidence to earn that degree of respect from your students which is essential to effective learning.

We are fortunate that scuba is such a unique pastime, involving personal entry into what is otherwise such an alien part of our planet. Exploring this otherwise closed part of our environment generates a special excitement. This produces an infectious passion for all things underwater in the scuba instructor, which must be passed on to the student. The enthusiasm so engendered in the student is a currency that the wise instructor will spend carefully. It will help the student to overcome fears, to persist when overcoming skill problems and to master difficult theoretical concepts. A good instructor will do everything possible to cultivate this natural enthusiasm resulting from the potential to explore an unknown world.

Instructor – Student relationship

Another aspect of instructing is the responsibility of supervising and directing the student's learning process. In an activity involving underwater swimming, it should go without saying that safety must always be paramount. This inevitably means the instructor must always be able to exercise an appropriate degree of control over the students.

Where scuba diving is being taught as a leisure activity, frequently being paid for by the student, the exercise of control must be earned through respect. Students will allow such control because they trust the instructor as a competent diver and as a reliable instructor, who in turn shows respect for their needs and feelings as students. A patient, sympathetic, professional approach is the hallmark of any instructor worthy of the title, whether paid or amateur.

Communication

Having an extensive repertoire of skill, knowledge and experience is something possessed by many divers. One thing that differentiates an instructor from a diver is the further ability to communicate this skill, knowledge and experience to students. So obviously communication skills are also a very necessary adjunct to the scuba instructor. Communication takes place at many levels and in a wide variety of situations. Many of these are discussed in detail later in this manual, and also form much of the subject matter of various instructor training events provided by the BSAC. Just as diving skills can be acquired, developed and polished, so too must prospective instructors learn and expand their communication capabilities.

Scuba is an activity open to all and students will come from all walks of life. They will show wide variety in age, temperament, academic background, swimming ability and personal aspiration. You will need to communicate and express yourself clearly, positively and concisely in a wide variety of teaching circumstances. A scuba instructor must be able to pass on knowledge in both formal and informal 'classroom' situations, in swimming pool and open water, above and below the surface. This demands a communication capability at least equal to the depth and breadth of the instructors' diving abilities.

Figure 1 Presenting scuba diving theory in a classroom.

Figure 2 An open water practical lesson on the use of the compass.

Assessing performance

Assessing and criticising a student's performance requires sensitivity and tact, if the student is not to lose self respect and confidence.

Try to remember some of the difficulties you experienced when you were at their level of training, this will often temper your impatience and consideration if the desired results are to be achieved. Avoid pressing them too hard or they will become disheartened and frustrated. It is often better to slow down the fast learners, but not to the extent that they become bored.

Your evident interest in sharing their progress and new experiences will enthuse your students to achieve their individual goals.

Attitudes

Whilst it is easy to have a positive attitude towards scuba diving, to be a successful instructor you must also have the right attitude towards teaching other people. Attitudes are personal traits resulting from the process of human development, and as such are very personal and difficult to change. Potential instructors must develop the right approach towards teaching the wide variety of students they will meet, or they are unlikely to be successful. The good instructor will derive as much pleasure from a student's mastery of a skill as the student themselves. Indeed, this is often the major part of their recompense! Obviously the instructors' personality reflects their attitudes towards their students. In this respect transparency, sociability, patience and a gentle sense of humour are all traits that will be appreciated by your students.

The instructor has a further important responsibility in developing in students the right attitudes towards underwater activities. Not only must you teach them to dive safely, but also to put safety first, to conserve and protect the underwater environment and to present a responsible image of scuba diving to the outside world.

The working instructor

There are a number of different teaching environments where scuba training is carried out:

BSAC Branches which are open to the general public, Special Branches where membership is restricted to people who are already part of a group; the military or employees of a company, University branches for students of a University, and School special branches for students of a school. Branches normally conduct their initial practical training during the evenings at a local swimming pool, and the theory sessions at their club house. Instruction at BSAC Schools is usually on a more regular basis, and caters for people who prefer to follow a course which takes place at a more convenient time i.e. during the day or at weekends. For example, schools can also offer concentrated courses for people who want to learn before going on a scuba diving holiday. Basic instruction usually takes place in a private or public swimming pool which can be indoors or outdoors, or in sheltered open water. Subsequently, open water training may progress to a lake or to a sheltered area of sea.

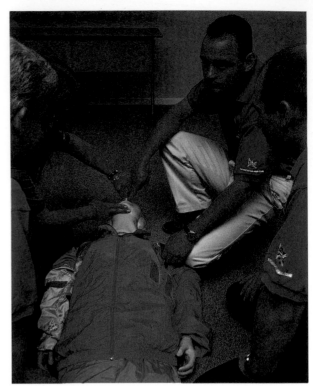

Figure 3 Lifesaving techniques can be taught effectively in a classroom environment.

Figure 4 Mask clearing under the watchful eye of the Instructor.

Teaching in all of these different environments will contribute to the qualities and skills needed by the "complete" instructor to use the facilities to their maximum advantage, and to obtain the very best from their students.

The working instructor – Branch

Once you have learnt the basic skills of good instructional technique, putting them to use is the only sure way of developing them further. Teaching in a variety of situations helps you to gain the broadest experience.

Teaching in a branch environment is generally wide-ranging, from basic pool instruction and theory lessons, to more advanced techniques in open water.

There is sometimes a tendency to consider the teaching of basic skills, such as finning and other surface skills, as being subordinate to scuba instruction. In fact, good instruction and technique at this early stage will endure throughout the students diving career, as will bad technique!

Pool instruction is often restricted to a one hour session, once a week, due to the demand from other pool users, or the expense of hiring the facility. In some instances, pool-time has to be shared with other activities such as swimming classes. Public swimming pools are generally not constructed with scuba training in mind. They can vary in shape, size, depth and temperature and it is not always possible to choose the ideal area to teach, both above and below the water. Therefore, your first priority is to maximize the available teaching time by planning your pool lessons in advance, and keeping briefings short and concise. Basic instruction is covered in more detail on pages 70-83.

Presenting theory lessons or lectures is probably more taxing in terms of facilities, for the branch instructor than pool training. Few Branches have dedicated classrooms where students can learn in an environment free from distractions – although there are some notable exceptions. Usually, Branch facilities have to be shared with other activities. Branch club houses range from accommodation in community centres, public houses, to purpose built facilities which may have more than one classroom.

Open water instruction, which is normally preceded by pool work and lectures, is usually organized at weekends, and is often combined with a general branch dive. Some Branches will put a day, or part of a day aside to teach open water skills, or to take students on their first dive.

Despite the possible lack of facilities and continuity in terms of training, branch instruction affords some of the best and most challenging territory for the would be instructor. Branch instruction produces some of the most varied and talented instructors, who become accustomed to improvisation and imaginative teaching.

Figure 5 Teaching the basics.

The working instructor – School

Teaching scuba in the world at large is on a far more commercial footing than the club-oriented style. Many divers overseas will do all their training through a School, often while on holiday and then only for two or three weeks a year. Even after many years of scuba diving, it is not unusual for them to dive with an instructor or guide from the School or Resort Centre and to have fairly low skill levels in dive organizing, planning, leading, navigating and problem solving. It is common for School instructors to spend a good deal of their time arranging and leading dives for groups of four or five customers taking on the responsibilities and role of a guide diver, rather than an instructor. These resort divers are looking for a safe, enjoyable underwater experience, often year after year, without the commitment demanded by advanced scuba training programmes.

Generally, Schools are better equipped in terms of classroom and pool facilities. They are often run in conjunction with a retail shop offering a range of scuba equipment for sale and hire. Schools situated in inland areas, and those located at coastal sites where the water temperature is too cold for initial training, usually hire pool- time in much the same way as Branches, although, a number do have purpose-built pools.

Schools situated in the tropics and near to the ocean take advantage of the warmer water, and use sheltered and accessible areas for teaching. Indeed, many warm water Schools perform all of their training in the sea. Many warm water Schools also conduct diving theory lessons in the open air, so that students and instructors benefit from the pleasant conditions.

As a School instructor you are likely to have responsibilities in addition to those of instruction. You may be required to fill customers' cylinders following training sessions, collect them from their arrival points, look after their domestic arrangements and, more importantly from the owner's point of view, advise on and sell equipment through the School's retail shop.

The notion that instructing professionally in a School is a glamourous and easy life is illusory. School instructors are always on demand, and can be required to dive several times a day, and just when you think you can rest, there is a promotional evening or someone wanting a night dive!

Resort centres and Schools often require instructors to speak an additional language, as their customers may be drawn from many different countries. As customers can have a variety of previous experience, it is essential for School instructors to have a very open approach and a wide knowledge of alternative training systems. Awareness of the major diver certification agencies and major national federations training schemes will be an obvious advantage.

Regardless of these additional pressures, teaching in a School can be a very rewarding experience. In particular it will help to improve your communicative skills and your understanding of the commercial pressures of being part of a business which survives on its reputation and customer satisfaction.

Figure 6 Instructor and students enjoying an underwater lesson in

warm clear water.

The Learning Process

The Learning Process

How we learn

Most learning is achieved through experience. The student needs to experience it themselves or they are less likely to learn, and this will limit the standards which can be reached. Therefore, you must provide the opportunities for students to experience and develop skills to an appropriate standard, and to know why the skills are necessary, as well as being able to perform them. Learning should also involve the what and why of the subject, not just the how.

It is possible for a student to go diving without knowing the theory, but they would have to obey the instructor's instructions closely, for example, breathe normally during the ascent. However, they would not have understood why they should do this (theory) – and without the 'what' and the 'why' they would be unsafe divers.

Safe and thorough learning involves the development of practical skills and the acquisition of the knowledge necessary to apply the skills, and to know exactly why they are being applied. Knowing how is only half the story. Knowing what and why quickly transforms the student into an accomplished and confident diver.

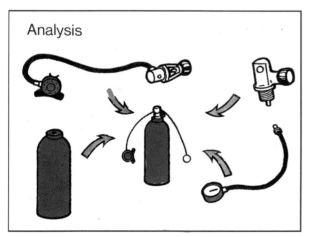

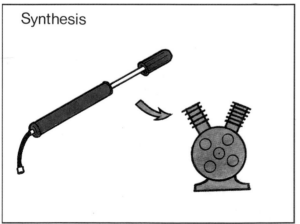

Figure 7 Learning by analysis and synthesis.

Students are the most important people in any training programme, and should not merely be fitted into an administratively convenient system. Students are also customers whose needs and aspirations must be satisfied. As instructors we need to teach in such a way that our students can clearly see that they are achieving their goals.

The structuring of organized experience is carried out through synthesis. This is the process of gradually building simple facts into more complicated relationships. Also through analysis, this is the breaking down of complicated systems into simple parts so that they can be more readily understood. See fig 7.

The process of synthesis can be exemplified by looking at the way in which a student gradually builds up an understanding of buoyancy from a number of isolated experiences. First that they can float, and then if weight is added, they sink. If they hold a full breath they float, and when they release it they sink. Added to this are the effects of pressure when they dive deeper than usual. The influence of the thickness of a wetsuit, of diving in salt or fresh water, and the effect of gradually consuming the air in their cylinder. These experiences do not happen all at once. It is only gradually that they become linked together as part of the total concept of buoyancy. Good instruction highlights relationships that link isolated facts into structured knowledge.

Analysis is the reverse of this process. When a student is faced for the first time with a new regulator, their previous experience suggests that it probably consists of several simple elements. On examination they look for evidence of the elements they expect to find and break the information into manageable parts. For example, how does the air enter the regulator? Is the regulator balanced or unbalanced? Is it a diaphragm or piston first stage? The student goes through a process, stage by stage, of making comparisons between facts that they discover, and knowledge that they already have.

Their intelligence allows them to make associations between facts, not only to see relationships that exist, but also to arrive at new relationships. Final understanding will only come from structured knowledge, and not from isolated pieces of information, no matter how well they are remembered.

Structured knowledge is essential to good recall or memory, as only when knowledge is structured will the recall of one fact bring to mind other facts related to it. An effective training programme must assist the students in obtaining an organized knowledge structure.

The senses

Learning, and hence knowledge, comes from the use of our senses – touch, sight, sound, taste and smell. In learning, the first three are the most important. However, if the word touch is used broadly to include doing, then sight combined with doing are the most powerful and important senses. Remember the adage – "I hear – I forget, I see – I remember, I do – I understand". See fig 8.

The more you allow and encourage your students to participate, the more they will remember.

For all able-bodied people sight is the most important sense but the relative importance between the senses does vary with individuals and with the task in hand. Information should be presented to students in a variety of forms so that it appeals to as many senses as possible, therefore making assimilation more effective. Learning takes place most effectively when a student consciously attends to the information that is being randomly fed to them through their senses, treats it selectively and structures it into an organized body of experience.

Motivation

For successful learning to take place the student must be motivated to learn and be sufficiently interested to give their attention to what is being taught. When students are motivated they will want to learn and eventually go scuba diving because they expect it to be enjoyable and exciting.

This initial interest and motivation should be continually stimulated by the instructor, otherwise disinterest and boredom will soon take their place. People can only assimilate facts and situations that they are aware of, and awareness depends on attention. We generally attend to situations in which we have an active interest or which impinge so vividly upon our senses that we are unable to ignore them. All instruction must therefore be made as interesting as possible, by careful use of material, and as vivid an experience as possible, by the use of the teaching techniques described later in this manual.

You can easily gain attention by using a loud voice or a threatening manner, but this will be of little lasting value compared to the attention gained by the instructor who fills their lesson with fascinating information delivered with a sense of humour. However, whilst jokes and a relaxed manner have their place, too much can transfer attention from the subject being taught to the performer, and the class remember the performance rather than the facts of the lesson. The student is most likely to remain interested through the more difficult topics if personal achievement shows them that they are making steady progress towards their goal. Success is important as it helps the student remember what they have learnt. This is because successful behaviour, satisfying as it does psychological needs, is reinforced or stamped more firmly into a person's behavioural patterns.

Progression

Progression implies a starting point and a direction. As instructors, we must design programmes which have structure with achievable steps. Progressive instruction introduces students to new learning in simple steps, through a planned programme of instruction which maintains their interest and confidence. This allows them to see that they are making progress towards self-imposed objectives.

Each new skill must commence at a point where it is linked to an existing skill and knowledge. This system applies to both learning in a classroom and to learning practical skills. It also includes opportunities for the instructor to check and correct their progress.

- **Seeing and doing**
  Combining sight with doing, particularly when teaching practical skills, is by far the most effective teaching method.
- **Hearing**
  During theory lessons, hearing is used extensively by most instructors. This sense should be supplemented with visual aids if the lessons are to be effective.

Other senses

- **Taste and Smell**
  Both these senses have a limited value in terms of scuba training.
- **Touch**

  All aspects of practical training involve touch. We can talk about and see the colour and shape of our diving cylinder, but we need to handle (touch) it to find out how heavy it really is.

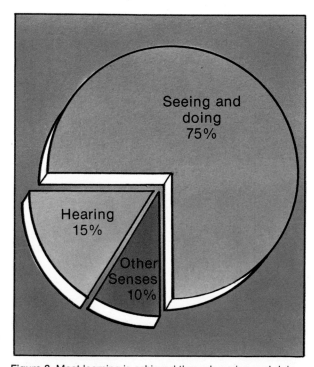

Figure 8 Most learning is achieved through seeing and doing.

By starting off from existing skills, the student progresses from the known to the unknown. See fig 11. The small steps are easily attainable objectives for the student, whereas if the whole complex skill were attempted in one giant stride it is unlikely that the student would succeed. This would lead to disappointment, frustration and lack of motivation.

For success in learning, the student must want to succeed; they must be allowed to succeed, and must know that they have succeeded; and their anxieties about their progress must be reduced. A feeling of progress satisfies the basic desire that is present in all of us to do well and this must be maintained. Students who reach a particular training objective need to be set another goal so that there is a feeling of continuous effort and progress towards their ultimate objective.

As the students' abilities and experience increase, larger steps can be taken to maintain the sense of challenge and to prevent boredom. At all times students need to be told how they are getting on, as knowledge of progress is an essential element to learning. To be effective, information on progress must be closely related to the moment of achievement, and performance needs to be discussed as soon as possible after the event.

There will inevitably be times when the student will feel that they are not making progress, when in fact they are. The instructor must constantly encourage them through these periods. Praise is more effective than criticism, so it is generally necessary to find something good to say about a particular performance.

There will however, be times when the student will not make any apparent progress and may on some occasions appear to lose ground. These periods are called "learning plateaus". See fig 10. Learning plateaus can occur for a number of reasons. It may be that the student has taken in sufficient material for their particular rate of mental assimilation, or in the case of physical skills, for their rate of muscular co-ordination, and is taking "time off" in order to adjust to this new information. It may be that they have just finished a period of poor instruction and that their motivation to learn has been diminished by the experience; it may be due to ill health, fatigue or that the student has reached their personal limitation. A good instructor will recognise these periods when they occur and will encourage their students through them, as enthusiasm will soon diminish if the student feels they are getting nowhere.

Under a progressive system of instruction the level at which a student learns can be increased. Human behaviour can be likened to an energy system, and like all energy systems, people tend to obey the law of least action and therefore expend no more energy than is absolutely necessary to overcome the immediate problem.

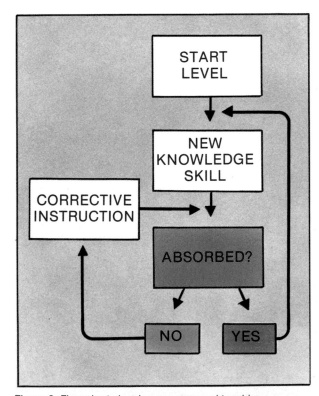

Figure 9 Flow chart showing programmed teaching.

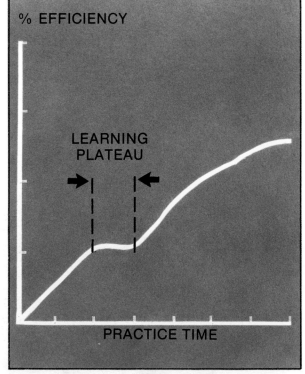

Figure 10 Theoretical learning Curve illustrating a learning plateau.

The more complex mental processes require greater energy on the part of the individual than do habitual responses, so there is a disinclination to employ them. If the instructor wants students to remember, imagine or reason with concentrated effort then they must arrange the learning environment in such a way that the extra effort demanded is worthwhile and satisfying to the students.

The level at which effort would normally cease can be raised by the presentation of a realistic and attainable challenge.

Good demonstrations will encourage a student to compare their own achievement with new standards. Therefore, the student becomes dissatisfied with their own attempts and is motivated to increase their own effort in order to attain the new level. If the standard is set too low, then the student will be easily satisfied and will not attempt to improve.

Programmed teaching

It is easy enough to present information and skills during your lesson but the important question is 'Are my students absorbing and understanding what I am teaching?'. If they are not, there may be little point in continuing with the instruction until their problems and misunderstanding are overcome. A lesson must include opportunities for the instructor to measure whether effective learning is taking place.

Programmed Teaching is a method which checks the students' performance and allows progress only when a previous piece of learning has been achieved.

It prevents building on a poor foundation and also serves to check your performance and effectiveness as an instructor. Programmed teaching techniques are easy to apply to practical lessons when errors in skill performance can be quickly spotted and corrected. It is not as easy to apply during theory teaching unless you are prepared to interrupt the flow of your lesson with questions or simple tests designed to see if learning has taken place.

Programmed teaching involves:

● Presenting your students with a package of knowledge or skill training.
● Analysing their knowledge or skill to see if they have absorbed the information.
● If they have, they can progress to the next package of learning.
● If they have not learnt, 2 is repeated (with emphasis on corrective instruction) to correct the skill and re-analyse it.

The process of programmed teaching is illustrated by a flow diagram in Figure 9 and for a practical lesson by Figure 15 on page 25.

Figure 11 Small steps are easily attainable, but if attempted in one giant stride it is unlikely the student would succeed.

Retention

The ability of your students to recall accurately the facts and skills they have been taught, is an important test of your effectiveness as an instructor.

Retention is closely related to the students' interest in both the instructor and the subject. If you present information in a less than enthusiastic manner, or demonstrate a skill which is poorly structured, your students will soon lose interest. Remember, students will not recall important information unless you have gained their interest and attention.

Interest can be held and recall improved if you state the objective and the reasons why the knowledge or skill is needed at the beginning of the lesson. Class involvement, enthusiasm, visual aids and an attention-holding presentation are good and effective elements in maintaining their interest.

Repetition also aids recall. For this reason, good training programmes are designed to include opportunities to repeat important skills. See fig 12. Mask clearing for example should be practiced regularly so that it becomes second nature. Similarly, essential information from your lecture should be repeated in the summary. Questioning is also helpful, as the memory is aided by frequent use.

Knowledge is more easily recalled when your students are personally involved in the reasoning process, rather than having the facts thrust upon them. Try to involve them in the progressive logic of the lesson. Where there are links between a number of facts, recall of one, leads quickly to recall of the others.

Attention

An important factor, closely related to the maintenance of interest, is the length of the teaching session.

Fatigue and boredom affect both the student and the instructor. It is essential that your material is relevant to the subject being taught and that your presentation is lively and holds their attention.

Mental fatigue comes as a result of intense or prolonged concentration, so where concentration is necessary the lesson should be brief, When either mental or physical tiredness is not excessive, your student will turn with interest from physical to mental activity and vice versa. This change of activity can make a refreshing alternative for your students. Rest periods can also be used to great effect during long sessions of learning. Attention varies from person to person, but as a general rule a normal period of learning falls into three phases. See fig 14.

The Introductory phase is a period of anticipation and interest, during which your students become more attentive as you introduce a new set of skill objectives or new information.

The main learning phase,when your students give

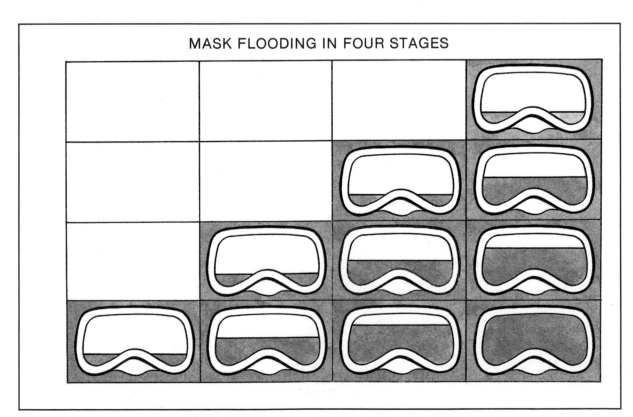

Figure 12 Good training programmes are designed to include opportunities to repeat important skills.

you their maximum attention. This phase can be extended or shortened depending on your ability to hold their attention.

The summary phase, when their interest climbs briefly in the knowledge that the lesson is nearly over. Use this period to good effect by summarizing the main points of your lesson. Try to avoid long and protracted teaching sessions. Your students will benefit more from small and effective teaching periods, where you inject variety and interest into your lessons. Better to teach a little well than a lot badly. For the average adult, periods of learning should not exceed 45 minutes. Remember, attention will also be affected by distractions, comfort, ventilation, temperature, lighting and other factors.

Learning can be defined as the acquisition of new knowledge and skills as a result of experience, in order to achieve personal objectives. A person's interest in taking up scuba diving may have been initiated by reading a book, watching a film, or seeing others enjoy the sport. In doing so they are establishing a personal objective – to learn to dive.

Most learning is achieved through experience. If the student does not experience it for themselves they are less likely to learn. As an instructor your role is to provide the opportunities for your students to experience and develop skills safely, and to an acceptable standard.

Figure 13 Learning is more effective when the students are involved in the learning process.

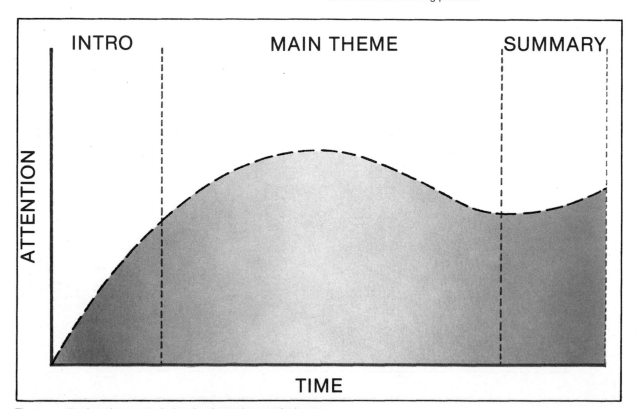

Figure 14 The learning curve during the three phases of a lesson.

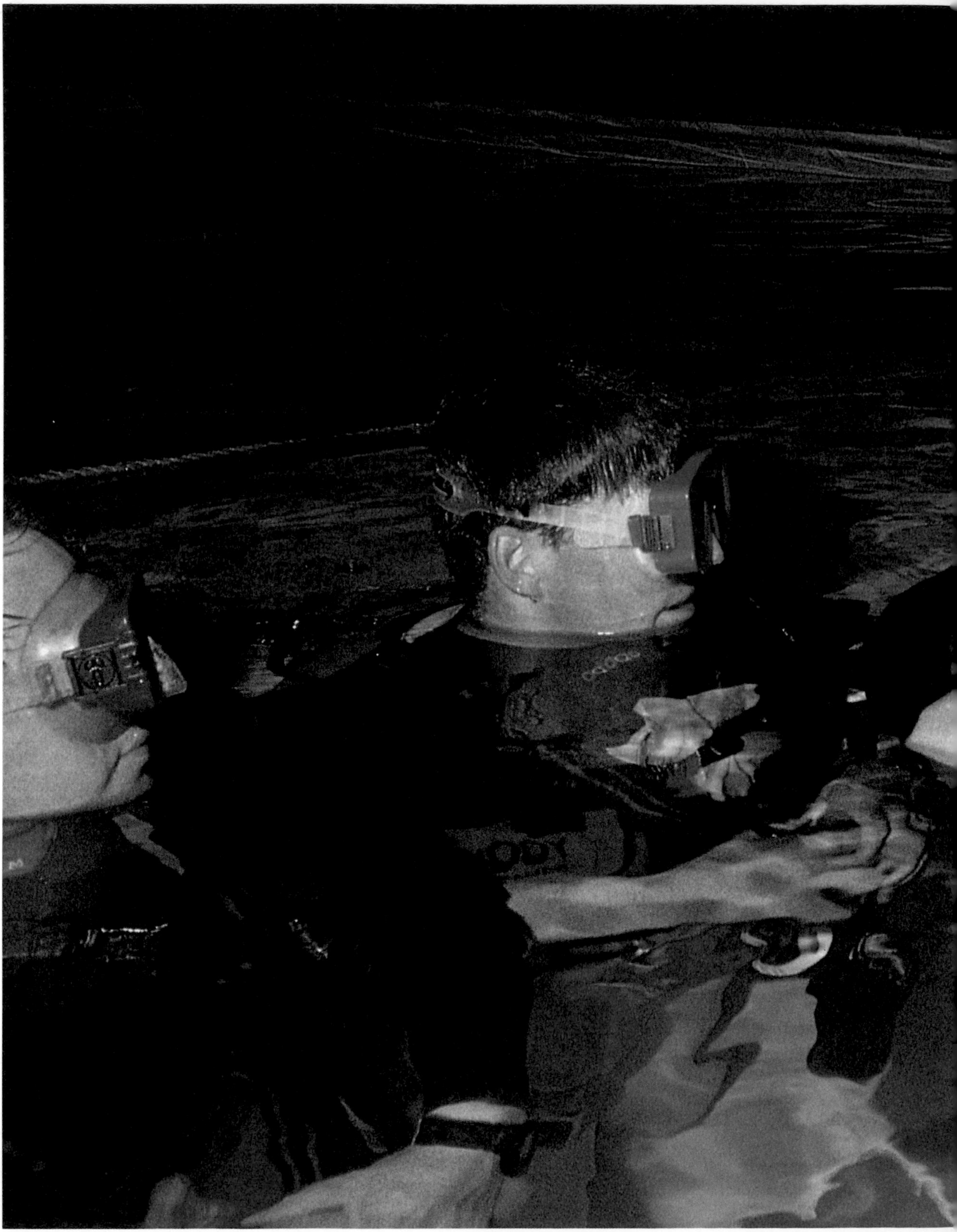

The Teaching Process

The Teaching Process

Learning is a voluntary act. It is impossible for you to force your students to learn, neither is it possible to draw up any relationship between the amount of learning that takes place in an instructional session and the amount of talking done by the instructor. The mere act of presenting information, even to a willing class, is not sufficient to ensure that learning will take place. Your prime role is to stimulate and to assist the learning process by creating the correct climate for learning, and then within this climate to communicate both knowledge and skill efficiently. In order to perform this task, you must acquaint yourself with the essential elements of the learning process and consider how best you can maintain and strengthen your students desire to learn. Then you should look at the techniques of communication most suited to achieving your objectives.

We saw in an earlier section on how learning depends upon initial motivation on the part of the student, the way in which this interest is maintained, and also how successful achievement of objectives will help to reinforce learning. To ensure that these essential elements are present in your teaching and that you can communicate information to your students in such a way that they can clearly understand and assimilate it, you must adhere to certain fundamental principles of teaching.

Aims and objectives

The aims and objectives of your teaching need to be clearly defined, or you will be unable to teach efficiently. For the student, these clearly defined objectives will indicate purpose, give confidence and will allow them to see clearly the goal they have to obtain. Once you have determined your objectives you must make a careful selection of the material that you are going to present. It is essential that this material is relevant to the objectives of the lesson, and that it is seen to be relevant by your students.

Attention is most sharply focused when the immediate value of what is being taught is fully understood. Once you have selected relevant material you must next organize it into a series of progressive steps suitable for presentation. These steps must be related to the developing experiences of the student, for relationships that are obvious to an experienced instructor may not be so readily apparent to the student. It is essential that progression through these steps be carefully graded, whether the material being taught is knowledge or physical skills. Through your selection of material you set a number of realistic levels of attainment for your students, high enough to enable them to extend their abilities, yet realistic enough to be within their grasp. Using this technique you can organize success into your instruction and minimize failure, this helps to maintain the motivation and interest of your students.

Pace and student involvement

When you are organizing the sequence of a presentation, give attention to the pace or the speed with which your students can grasp and assimilate each new step as this will determine the amount of practice and repetition needed, which will in turn influence the number of teaching sessions required to cover the selected material.

For a student to learn, they have to make a positive effort to acquire and retain knowledge and this is greatly assisted when they become personally and actively involved in the learning process. It is important that you organize this active involvement into your teaching. All students consciously desire to make progress and this is only satisfied by the knowledge that progress is being made. All instruction must include some means by which the student can judge their progress. Your role is also to ensure that the student is constantly informed of the progress they are making. For knowledge and skills to be of any real value, they must be retained and understood. This necessitates planned revision as well as the use and application of new skills and knowledge. It is not sufficient that you carefully present a unit of material, you must also see that this is periodically reviewed and practiced until it has become fully assimilated into the total body of the students' experience. Finally, no matter how carefully material is selected, arranged and repeated all will be to no avail unless efficient communication is established. These essential teaching principles can be summarized as follows:-

● Define clearly the purpose and objectives of teaching in terms of student attainment.

● Select teaching material carefully having regard to its relevance, degree of difficulty and progression.

● Plan to involve the student actively in the learning process.

● Ensure that the student is kept aware of their progress.

● Plan revision and practice to ensure assimilation.

● Use efficient methods of communication.

To put these general principles into practice you must:-

● Plan carefully the overall scheme of instruction.

● Prepare fully each separate unit of instruction.

● Present your material efficiently.

The basic concept centres around the three P's: Concentrating on the first two will make the third much easier!

Planning
Preparation
Presentation

Lesson planning

The acquisition of knowledge and technique is an organic process in which the various elements are inter-related and inter-dependent. Before you can prepare in detail a particular instructional session, its relationship to the overall training programme must be established. A training programme must therefore be first blocked out in broad terms to ensure that knowledge and skills are being presented in a suitably developing sequence.

Starting with the students' initial experience, each subsequent session must build upon the work that has preceded it, and each session must prepare the way for the next. In scuba diving, where theoretical knowledge and physical skills combine to give proficient technique, theory and practice must develop together. Care must be taken to ensure that there are opportunities to put theory into practice and that there is adequate practical experience from which to develop new theory. This can best be done by listing the factual and skill content relevant to each stage of the training programme and then placing them in order of dependence. Initial planning must also determine that the training programme will succeed at the correct pace. If a programme moves too slowly, the students will lose interest and become bored. If it moves too rapidly they will lose confidence in their ability to succeed.

After each session in the programme the students must feel that they have made a positive step forward, either by the acquisition of some new knowledge or skill, or by the fact that they have consolidated, perfected or applied some previously acquired experience.

In all training programmes, time is limited so it is essential to choose the most efficient presentation technique available e.g. lecture, lesson, discussion, informal talk, demonstration or film. The relative merits of these techniques will be discussed later in this manual. Variation in technique during the programme will add variety and bring added student stimulation. Where a number of individuals excel at particular techniques of presentation they can be encouraged to develop topics best suited to their skills.

Time for revision and the checking of progress must also be planned into the programme. Progress can be checked by formal testing, or it can be tested less formally e.g. Quiz games, discussion groups, simulated planning exercises. All of these will give your students the opportunity to display their knowledge and also afford opportunity for revision. Team competitions allow practical abilities to be demonstrated. The following steps should be considered when planning your lesson:-

● A clear statement in terms of knowledge or physical skills that your student should have achieved at the end of the lesson.

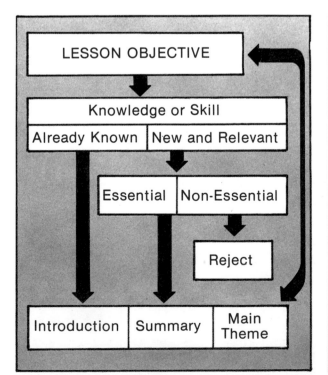

Figure 15 Typical lesson format.

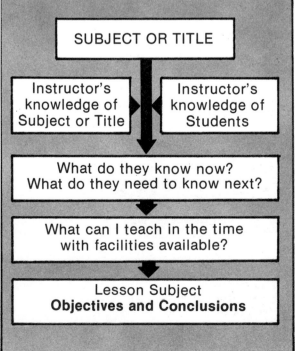

Figure 16 Define the lesson objectives early in lesson planning.

- A full analysis of the facts and skills needed to achieve this.
- A consideration of the techniques available for communicating these facts and skills.
- A decision as to how student achievement can best be measured.

An important step in lesson planning is to make sure that you teach what the student needs to know about the subject at this stage of their training, therefore it is important to design your lesson around the students' needs, not around the lesson title. You should also attempt to teach only what your students need to know in order for them to reach their objective; usually the next diver qualification level. In this planning phase where the broad aims of the teaching session are decided and outlined, it is important that you also address the following questions in order to plan an effective lesson:-

Who?
What is the current level of knowledge or skill of the students?.
Am I talking to people with an expert understanding of related subjects or is this subject all very new to them?

What?
What is the subject? What do my students already know and what do I want them to know when I have finished? What facilities will be available?

How?
How many people am I talking to?
Large numbers normally dictate a more formal approach: small numbers can allow more class participation.
Audience size will also influence the choice of visual aids.

Preparation
Once the broad pattern for the lesson has been established you will be able to start the detailed planning of each session. You should begin by establishing a specific aim for the session which should take into account the standard of the students being taught, together with the time and the facilities that are available. It is not really possible, for example, to teach snorkel diving techniques effectively unless there is a suitable pool and time for pool practice available, nor can 'Navigation' be taught in a single forty minute session.

The aim for a particular session must be specific since it is possible to teach a given title at many different levels. The particular level must depend upon the experience of your students at that stage.

Figure 17 Lesson notes keep your presentation on track.

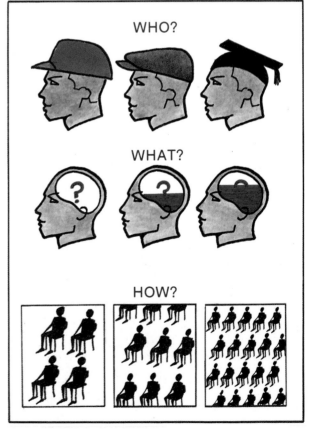

Figure 18 Who, What and How.

"To introduce the reasons for decompression illness and to outline the symptoms by which it can be recognised" is a specific aim. This limits you to an elementary explanation of conditions that can induce decompression illness and the ways by which a diver suffering from this illness can be recognised. It does not necessitate the discussion of controversial theories nor does it require an explanation of the ways by which the condition can be treated. More advanced theories can wait until your students have had time to read up on the subject and assimilate a greater background experience. First aid and recompression treatment of the condition can also come in a later session.

Aims and objectives

The purpose of a training session can take a number of forms, e.g. to teach the understanding of a principle; to teach the correct way to physically carry out a skill; to teach how something works; but in every case the aim should pass the test of being relevant, definite and limited. It is quite obvious when an instructor is not perfectly clear about the objectives from the unstructured nature of their material and the way in which they are easily distracted from their theme by the class.

The objective of a session, being class related, determines the next step in preparation which is the selection of suitable teaching material. After you have structured your overall lesson it is important to collect and organize as wide a range of relevant source material as possible. It is advisable to build up a reference library of books,

magazines, lesson notes and cuttings which you can call upon in your preparation.

The rapid growth of knowledge and changing practices makes it unwise to rely upon one or two textbooks for information. It is essential that all your information is as up to date as possible and is technically accurate.

This collection will obviously contain far more material than can, or should, be presented to your students, therefore your preparation should involve the process of selection.

Your material should be limited to the lesson objective and you should avoid the temptation to include too much material. Start by enumerating the essential points to be made if the aim is to be achieved and then choose material to suit the standard of class, their experience and the time available.

The material being selected can usefully be considered under four headings:-

● Facts that are essential and the student **must** know at this stage.
● Facts which the student **should** know.
● Facts which the student **could** know if time permits.
● Facts which are not relevant at this stage and can be safely left out.

Grading factual material in this way has the practical advantage of helping the inexperienced instructor overcome the fear of 'drying up' and therefore including an excessive amount of material in the preparation.

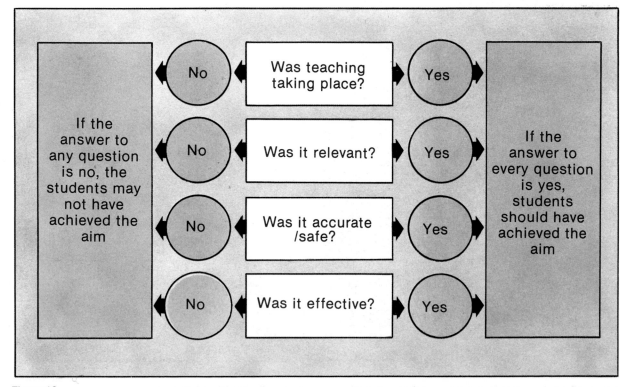

Figure 19

OXYGEN ADMINISTRATION

LECTURE NOTES:

Introduction (5 minutes)

● What is Oxygen? *(show visual aid of title)*

● Oxygen forms 21% of the air we breathe. *(show visual aid of pie chart)*

● Oxygen is non-flammable but will support combustion.

● Oxygen is tasteless, colourless and odourless.

● Oxygen is essential to LIFE!

Main Theme (20 minutes)

● The role of Oxygen in respiration. *(use diagram)*

● ....

Figure 20 Lesson notes ensure that the essential information is covered.

Your initial intention should be to conclude the session having covered the "must know" and "should know" facts. If you find that you have some time left then the "could know" facts can be used to fill it. However, if your presentation takes longer than you anticipated, you know what the essential minimum is that needs to be covered to achieve your objectives.

Notes

Once the content of your session has been decided it is advisable to prepare notes to ensure that essential material is not forgotten during the presentation, and also to ensure that statements are factually correct. Avoid notes that have been written out too fully as they can prove difficult to follow, and the inexperienced instructor will usually end up reading from them, this can lead to a dull presentation. Notes can initially be prepared in full, but it is then advisable to edit them so that they contain only the important information. In this way it is the essential points that stand out clearly and the instructor can talk around them while still following a logical progression. Write your notes out legibly, preferably on small cards for use as memory aids and prompts. It is useful to underline or highlight key words and phrases so that they can be seen at a glance.

Presentation

Having determined your objectives and selected the material that you wish your students to learn, you can now begin to prepare your presentation.

The relaxed and confident manner of the experienced instructor often belies the careful thought that has gone into producing an apparently effortless performance. Good instructional technique requires that every possibility, from the choice of instructional method to the availability of a board marker and cleaner, has been considered. Most periods of instruction will fall into three phases:-

Introduction
Development
Conclusion

Introduction

The main purpose of the introductory phase is to place before the student the intention of the instructor and to prepare their minds to receive the new material. Remember, that prior to your teaching session your students may have been engaged in other activities, swimming in the pool, listening to a lecture on a different topic or travelling from home or work. Time will be needed for them to orientate to the topic that you are going to present and to adjust from their previous activity. The time spent on the introductory period must not be too long and can be regarded as a warming up period to the main activity of the session. The introduction may, in some instances, be just part of a brief statement of intention on the part of the instructor or a brief outline of the subject to be covered.

Knowledge, however, is more easily recalled if it is structured and this introductory period can be well used to forge a link between the new material and some previous knowledge. Where the session is one of a series on related topics, this time can be spent usefully in a brief revision of the previous topics to refresh memories before moving on.

This opening period is important as it is at this time that you establish your relationship with your class. It is essential that it flows smoothly to give an immediate impression of preparedness and confidence and to awaken the interest of your students. This is the time to lay a good foundation from which the rest of the session can develop.

Avoid over-confidence and too rapid a pace at the start. Make sure you have the students' attention, give them time to orientate to the subject and then quicken the pace of presentation. Some instructors, wishing to commence in a relaxed atmosphere, start in a light-hearted manner with an anecdote or joke. Be sure of the story if you are going to attempt this as there is nothing so flat as a joke that does not raise a laugh.

Development

The development phase is the period during which the main teaching material is presented. To ensure that this is developed in the most effective sequence there are a few principles that you should adhere to. The starting point is the knowledge already possessed by the class; the new knowledge is developed from this. Progression should be from the known to the unknown; from the simple to the complex; from the particular to the general. The pace of development and the number of new facts that are introduced must be related to the experience and ability of the group. Essential facts need to be returned to during this phase to ensure that they are reinforced and the instructor must be prepared to explain a point in a different way if the initial explanation is not clearly understood.

It is far better that a little is taught well than a lot which is poorly understood. In your preparation of this phase consider how you can introduce variety into your presentation. Consider what the students will be doing and remember that listening soon becomes boring. Remember we receive 75% of our information through the sense of sight and only 15% through the hearing sense.

For communication to be truly effective the spoken word needs to be supplemented with visual material; it is often said that "a picture is worth a thousand words". The use of visual material brings added interest to the lesson and provides a focal point for the students' attention. There are many aids available to the instructor and these are discussed on pages 56-67 in this manual, but to be effective the material and its use must be carefully planned. The amount used must be carefully chosen to make just the right point; too much is as bad as none at all. It is of little use showing a large number of irrelevant slides just because they happened to be available. Visual material needs to be examined closely to see that it does emphasize or clarify the point to be made. Some charts, for example, only serve to confuse, as they carry too much detail which is irrelevant to the scuba diver.

It is essential that a visual aid is on hand when it is needed. There is nothing more distracting than searching around for missing material as this will break into the flow of the lesson. Visual material also needs to be kept out of sight until it is needed otherwise attention will be diverted to it.

No matter how good a presenter you are or how well your presentation is supported with visual material, you must remember that learning is most efficient when the student is actively involved in the process. Your planning must take account of this and provide opportunity for student involvement where possible. Questions properly used make the student think for themselves; they can be given apparatus to handle or be given facts and shown how to draw conclusions from them. It is far better that students be encouraged to find out things for themselves and discover principles under guidance than for them to be continually presented with facts to assimilate.

Figure 21 Using the 'real' thing as a visual aid to hold the class' attention.

Conclusion

The final phase of the session is the conclusion. Too often this important phase is not properly utilized and an instructional session just fizzles out. This phase is important because towards the end of a session there tends to be an increase in the attention level of the class, possibly in anticipation of the break that follows. Now is the time to reiterate the main points that need to be made and to push them home. This may be done with a point-by-point summary by the instructor or by guided questioning around the class. Added value comes from this if the summary is accompanied by a visual presentation in the form of a board summary of the key words, labels added to a diagram, or a reference to the parts of actual equipment.

As knowledge is structured the final phase of the session can prepare the ground for the introduction phase of the next session in the series. Reading can be suggested or the students can be left with a question, the answer to which forms the starting point of the next lesson or session. Finally, it is essential to leave some time for questions from the students, if their interest has been stimulated during the session they will be keen to find out more.

Although instructional sessions all tend to follow this general pattern of introduction, development and conclusion, the facts, skills and ideas which they aim at communicating can be delivered by a number of different and varied techniques. The techniques most likely to be encountered in diving instruction are the lecture, lesson, discussion, open forum, tutorial and the instructors practical demonstration.

Getting started

One of the most common difficulties encountered by would be presenters is the initial nervousness they feel when they stand up to address an audience. It is worth mentioning here that naturally gifted and completely relaxed presenters are very rare indeed and even the most experienced of instructors will admit to feeling some apprehension when about to present a lesson. This is quite normal and, in fact, some instructors believe that the adrenaline produced in such situations actually enhances their performance.

Remember that your audience is highly unlikely to know as much about the subject as you do. To help overcome initial nerves it is worthwhile preparing and rehearsing the opening stages of a presentation particularly well, even to the point where the first few minutes are learnt by rote, in a similar fashion to the lines in a play. This will allow you to concentrate on other aspects of the lesson such as your voice and the pace of your delivery. Getting the presentation off to a good start will increase both your confidence and the chances of the entire presentation being a success. For example, if you are teaching a group which you are meeting for the first time, you might want to introduce and outline your credentials applicable to teaching the topic. This should not be regarded as 'blowing ones own trumpet' but rather as both a courtesy and a means of inspiring confidence in the students, who after all, will surely want to feel that they are in safe and knowledgeable hands.

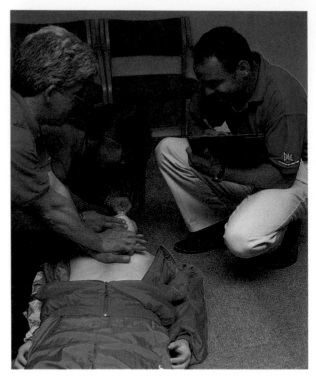

Figure 22 Students practically involved with the lesson – Artificial Ventilation.

Although it is easier said than done, try to remain relaxed and natural and make best use of the principle tools of the presenter, the voice and the eyes. Using your voice correctly can enliven the most dry technical subject, conversely a flat, monotone voice can send the most ardent student to sleep in no time at all. First of all ensure that everyone in the audience can hear and see you. There are two possibilities here, simply ask whether those towards the back of the room can hear and see you clearly? Or, alternatively, a fellow instructor sitting at the back of the room can signal you to increase or decrease the volume of your voice. Try and speak clearly without mumbling and vary the pace, pitch and timbre of the voice to add interest, to emphasize specific and important areas of the presentation and to keep the class awake. Stage actors rely heavily on their voices for impact and an instructional presentation could be regarded in just the same way, as a stage performance. Try to use standard English and minimize the use of regional or colloquial expressions. If you happen to have a strong regional dialect it is even more important to speak clearly and slowly enough so that everyone can understand what you are saying. Learning diving theory is complex enough without expecting your students to carry out simultaneous translation as you speak.

A common fault induced by nervousness is to fix on a specific spot, the visual aid or chalkboard, one sympathetic looking individual in the audience, the front row of faces or, some inanimate object like a crack in the ceiling or wall.

A skilled presenter will try to make deliberate and direct eye to eye contact with each and every student in the class at some stage during the presentation. Not surprisingly this is known as 'eyeball contact' and it serves several important functions. Firstly, it helps to make each student feel more involved in the lesson as it sends the message to each that they are being addressed personally by the presenter. Secondly, it minimizes the opportunities for a students' attention to start wandering. Finally, it helps you to monitor the reactions of the class to the lesson.

Unless you are delivering a formal lecture to a very large group, in which case you might be forced to operate from behind a lectern on a raised platform or stage, then every effort should be made to keep reasonably close to the audience and eliminate physical barriers such as lecterns and desks. A common fault, which again is an understandable response to nervousness, is for the presenter to retreat behind some physical barrier, like a desk, in the belief that this provides some form of defence against an audience who are perceived as being hostile, even if they are not.

Standing in front of the class in an open space helps the presenter to develop a better rapport with the class and creates more of a relaxed, friendly and informal atmosphere in which the student is more likely to learn. There is however a danger that in attempting to create a more relaxed and informal environment the presenter goes too far and loses some of the important psychological advantages that should be maintained between instructor and student.

In a classroom teaching environment examples of being perhaps too relaxed might be, sitting on a table with legs swinging, sitting down in a chair or leaning against the chalkboard etc. A friendly, relaxed and approachable style are all desirable attributes of the good instructor but there should never be any doubt as to who is the instructor in the class.

The instructor/presenter therefore needs to establish and maintain a slightly dominant demeanour and posture relative to the students. This should be rather subtly achieved, it does not have to be overt or aggressive. Standing, rather than sitting, in front of a group of seated students should create the desired effect. Avoid being too dominant, for example, invading the students 'personal space' by standing too close to them is an aggressive act which may promote anxiety and reduce your teaching effectiveness.

Mannerisms

Most instructors have mannerisms by which their students recognise them, and these are not important unless they develop to a degree where they distract attention from what is being taught. Throwing chalk into the air, tapping with a pencil, fiddling with keys or coins in the pocket can all become annoying after a time. Nervous verbal habits also interfere with communication and hesitant 'ums' and 'ers' and the repetition of phrases such as 'you see' cause irritation. However, everyone has some personal peccadilloes, habits and mannerisms, after all these are what make people individuals.

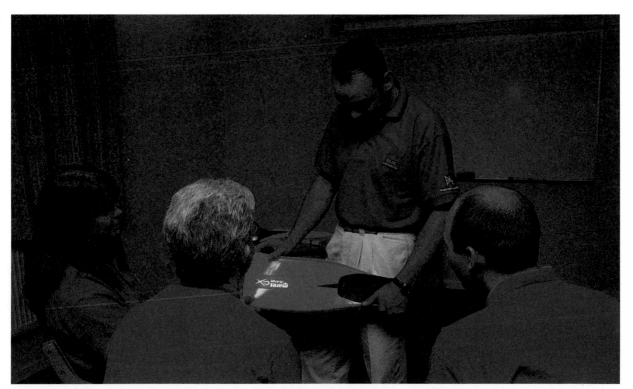

Figure 23 Standing rather than sitting in front of a seated class establishes the student/instructor relationship.

Often these mannerisms are reactions to anxiety and stress, common examples might be covering ones mouth with a hand when speaking to someone who is a bit intimidating, or wringing one's hands. Unfortunately, because giving a presentation can be reasonably stressful, some of these mannerisms can be amplified and become too obvious to the audience. Apart from the amusement this might cause at the expense of the presenter, the real detriment is that the class become focused upon the mannerism and stop listening to the content of the lesson, thus defeating the teaching objective.

Mannerisms common to instructors giving presentations include:-

fiddling with the bezel of a diving watch, twiddling a dress ring, juggling with the chalk, rattling coins in a pocket, continually extending and retracting the board pointer, repetitive, compulsive and unnecessarily straightening of the transparencies on the OHP, excessive pacing, nose tweaking, hair stroking, lip licking, scratching, excessive gesturing with hands and arms, mumbling, grunting, saying 'er' and 'um' after every other word, talking to the board etc; the list is endless.

It is possible to take precautionary steps to avoid some of these potential distractions, for example removing your wristwatch and placing it where it can be seen but not easily touched, removing the coins from your pockets etc.,

The instructor is usually completely unaware of their own personal mannerisms until they are pointed out, so this is once more a good argument for having a friend, ideally another sympathetic and experienced instructor who knows what to look for, to sit in on your presentations to provide feedback to you in this area. As long as any mannerisms you tend to exhibit are minor, and do not detract from your teaching, then they can be ignored. If, however, they are a significant distraction then you must make a conscious and deliberate effort to eliminate them, at least whilst you are presenting.

Use of questions

A technique which needs considerable practice is the use of questions during instruction, as this is the most direct way of involving students in the instruction process. Questions must be selected carefully and examples of types that should be avoided are: those which have an obvious answer; elliptical questions such as, "pressure can effect the ear-drums, can't it?" pointless questions such as, "Do you see what I mean?". Avoid rhetorical and meaningless questions such as "Do you understand?", this would usually invoke a nodding response or a "yes" from the class, which in itself is totally meaningless. Avoid posing questions which are intended to trick or confuse the class, either because they are deliberately misleading or very difficult. It is worthwhile during preparation to consider how questions can be used to stimulate a short discussion, lead the class to discover a principle for itself, revise points already made, or awaken an inattentive student.

Any question posed should be directly relevant to information which the students have been given and therefore should be capable of being answered correctly by anyone in the class. Questions correctly answered act as a confidence booster to the students. Being asked a question which they cannot answer is a definite demotivator. When you use questions you should first address them to the class as a whole to make each member start thinking towards the answer. After a short pause ask one person, by name, to answer. Phrase your questions clearly and space them well around the class to keep all students alert.

Be prepared to handle wrong answers. If these are curtly dismissed the student in error will be discouraged from trying another time; it may be possible to develop a point from a wrong answer. Use wrong answers to judge the effect of your teaching and in particular the clarity of your explanations, since it may not be the student who is at fault. Whether you have been asking questions of the students or not during the presentation, it is a good idea, and a courtesy, at the conclusion of the session to ask whether your students wish to ask you any questions relative to the lesson. This is their opportunity to ask for clarification or further explanation. Try and deal with such questions accurately and sympathetically. If you don't know the answer to a question then do not try to waffle your way through, clearly state that you are not sure of the answer but will undertake to find out within a specified length of time. You will not lose credibility by adopting this approach, you gain it.

Written handouts are often a good way of further reinforcing the teaching you have given during your presentation. Obviously if you are going to use these then they need to be carefully planned and prepared in advance of the presentation. Handouts should at least emphasize and summarize the important "must know", "should know" information contained in the lesson.

Additionally, the handout might quote reading references in other diving manuals and publications which are relevant to the lesson topic. During the actual presentation of the lesson your handouts, like your other visual aids, should be kept out of sight. Distribute these only at the end of the lesson. See fig 24.

Positioning

Your position is very important, for instance, when a freestanding board or screen is being used, it will be most convenient for a right-handed person to position the board on their left as they face the class. This will enable you to turn easily towards the board when you need to write on it or to use a pointer on a screen.

Give some attention to your stance. In normal teaching it is unwise for you to be seated during a presentation. You should stand easily in front of your group but must avoid the habit of pacing about like a caged lion. Some movement is acceptable, but excessive movement should be avoided by planning the arrangement of any teaching aids so that they come readily to hand.

Finally, remember that teaching is a skill and like all other skills it will improve with dedication and guided practice.

After a while, apprehension will diminish and performance can be polished. Do not be afraid to ask for help, an experienced instructor can offer useful advice to the beginner if they are asked to sit in on a session and comment afterwards on its effectiveness. An instructor can also help themselves by examining their own performance to see why it failed or succeeded. Such questions as:-

- Did I cover the essential facts?
- Could I have made my points more clearly?
- Was I distracting my audience?
- Were the visual aids I used adequate?
- Did I go on talking too long?
- Do I need to change anything?

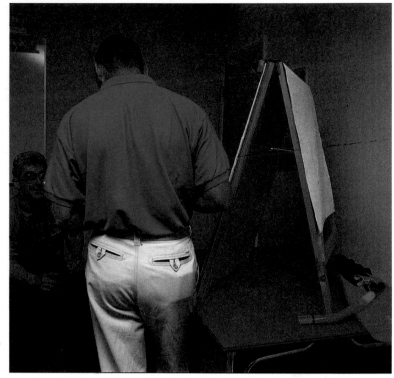

Figure 24 Keep your handouts or visual aids out of sight until required.

Figure 25 Try to avoid sitting, slouching, or pacing up and down during your lecture.

Practical Teaching

Practical Teaching

Scuba diving is essentially a practical activity requiring a combination of theoretical knowledge and skill behaviour, which together build good technique. Besides being able to teach the theoretical knowledge associated with diving, the scuba instructor must understand how skill behaviour is acquired.

Teaching good habits

People are born with a limited number of reflex actions and have the ability to develop a limitless range of adaptive behavioural patterns. They continually acquire habits, adapt them to new situations, and add them to their skills.

A habit is a learned response to a given situation, where a similar behaviour pattern persists over a considerable period without modification. Each time the particular situation occurs, the behaviour pattern exhibits a similar form and serves a similar function.

Habitual behaviour of this sort is an essential element in scuba diving and divers under instruction must be taught a number of habits which will serve them well throughout their scuba diving career. If habits are examined more closely, it will be seen that they are not absolutely rigid, but do tend to become generalised in the form they take, e.g. the habit is to check, what is checked and how it is checked can differ. Because of this, it is possible for people to adapt their habitual behaviour to suit particular situations and circumstances, however if habits are to be adapted in this way, they must be supported by sound knowledge.

The snorkel diver who understands the principles behind the performance of a surface dive can soon adapt this basic skill to suit the occasion when they are carrying a camera or are diving in restricted conditions. It is this ability to adapt behaviour that forms the basis for the complex organization of physical and mental activity which we know as skill.

Skill learning

Divers are mainly concerned with motor skills, that is, a number of complex movements that are carried out without conscious attention on their part.

Observation of a mixed ability group performing a physical task will soon reveal two distinct levels of activity. The inexperienced will be seen to concentrate upon the task in hand, aware of everything they do, their actions being consciously controlled. The experienced, on the other hand, will perform smoothly and without conscious effort. Their behaviour has become habitual.

Although the increased smoothness of performance that comes with practice is the most obvious indication of skill development, there is another less obvious, but all important factor. The overall performance of a skill depends on the order in which its various parts are performed. Some are quite rigid, others flexible. Someone under instruction will follow fairly rigid patterns of activity. This is possible because the circumstances vary only slightly each time the skill is attempted.

On the other hand, the sequence of actions required in a complex skill, such as a lifesaving situation, can only be predicted in the early stages of training. In reality, the skilled lifesaver has to adapt rapidly to changing circumstances and works only within a broad pattern. This ability of the skilled person to make rapid and integrated responses to a changing situation, is an impressive part of the skilled performance.

Learning by doing

Skills are essentially learnt by carrying out the task. Normally, sight is the most important sense by which information is obtained, but in skill learning the actual use of the muscles is three times as important as seeing the skill performed. Listening to a detailed account of how the actions should be performed is of even less value than watching a performance. However, where possible, the demonstration of a skill should be accompanied by a verbal description of its finer points which explains the detail to help understanding. Ability in a skill can only be developed through controlled practice of the skill itself.

A student could be allowed to experiment for themselves and through trial and error, discover how to perform the skill. However, this sort of uncontrolled learning is time consuming, unprofitable and frustrating. While a student might attain some degree of success by teaching themselves, it is almost certain that they will in the process pick up a number of incorrect techniques. Muscle memory is more durable than factual memory and our self-taught student will find it difficult to break incorrect habits when an instructor comes along to improve their technique.

'Unlearning' is a difficult process; anyone who has attempted to learn the front crawl stroke after being well practiced in the breast stroke will remember how the old leg kick interfered with the new one. This interference brings reduced performance levels until the new actions are mastered.

Dissatisfaction with the apparently poorer performance causes the student to revert to their earlier style, which although ultimately less efficient, brings a greater feeling of success at this point. Skill learning needs clear demonstration to ensure that correct patterns of action are seen and practiced from the start to minimize the necessity for any 'unlearning'.

The progress a student will make towards the acquisition of a skill depends upon a number of factors. The first of these does not really come under the control of the instructor. Skills involve muscular dexterity involving the close co-ordination of mind and muscle, thus the performance of an individual will be greatly affected by their personal ability. This ability will vary from individual to individual and you must be prepared for the student who is 'all thumbs'. Good instruction can ensure that each student is encouraged to make the most of their natural ability by paying close attention to the other factors affecting their progress.

These factors are;

● the degree to which the student is able to understand.
● the nature of the activity they are being asked to imitate.
● the complexity of this activity.
● the standard of performance that they are given as an example to imitate.

The sequential nature of some activities make it possible for them to be easily broken down into a series of discrete actions, and a good level of performance can be achieved by teaching the elements of the activity as drills. This is fine when 'doing things by numbers', such as the procedure for starting a compressor. It allows less experienced students to safely follow a routine, but this method does have its disadvantages if followed blindly and without thought.

Too rigid adherence to drills in any training programme can produce habits which lack the necessary knowledge content that lies behind true skilled behaviour. Drills will produce predictable behaviour patterns in a given situation but these tend to be sterile and hinder the students' ability to adapt to changing conditions. Understanding the true nature of a skill comes from guided imitation where explanation helps understanding and brings with it insight into the true nature of the activity.

Complex skills

A slower learning rate is generally associated with the skills becoming more complex, and you need to consider how far a complex skill can be usefully broken down into minor elements. When this procedure is deemed necessary, you should decide how far each teaching unit will continue to interest the student. Take care in selecting the units to ensure that each of the several minor skills that are involved all fit naturally into their developmental sequence when the complex skill is practiced as an integrated system.

The development of a complex skill by teaching its parts can be done in two ways;

● sequentially, when the first element is practiced first, then the second added and the two elements practiced together, then the third added to the first two elements and so on.

● or by practicing each element independently of the others and then finally combining all the practiced elements into the complete skill.

Basic skills can be taught sequentially, e.g. mask clearing; mask clearing and regulator clearing, regulator clearing and buoyancy control, etc. Lifesaving skills can be taught as a series of elements, e.g. towing, artificial ventilation, equipment removal, landing techniques; to be finally combined into the total lifesaving procedure.

The method chosen will depend upon the nature of the skill, but in any programme of instruction it is essential to see that opportunities for success are built into each progressive stage of the exercise.

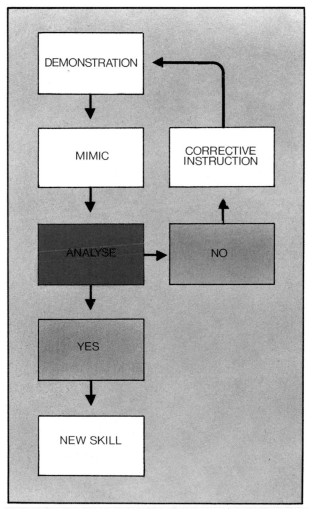

Figure 26 Flow chart of a practical lesson plan.

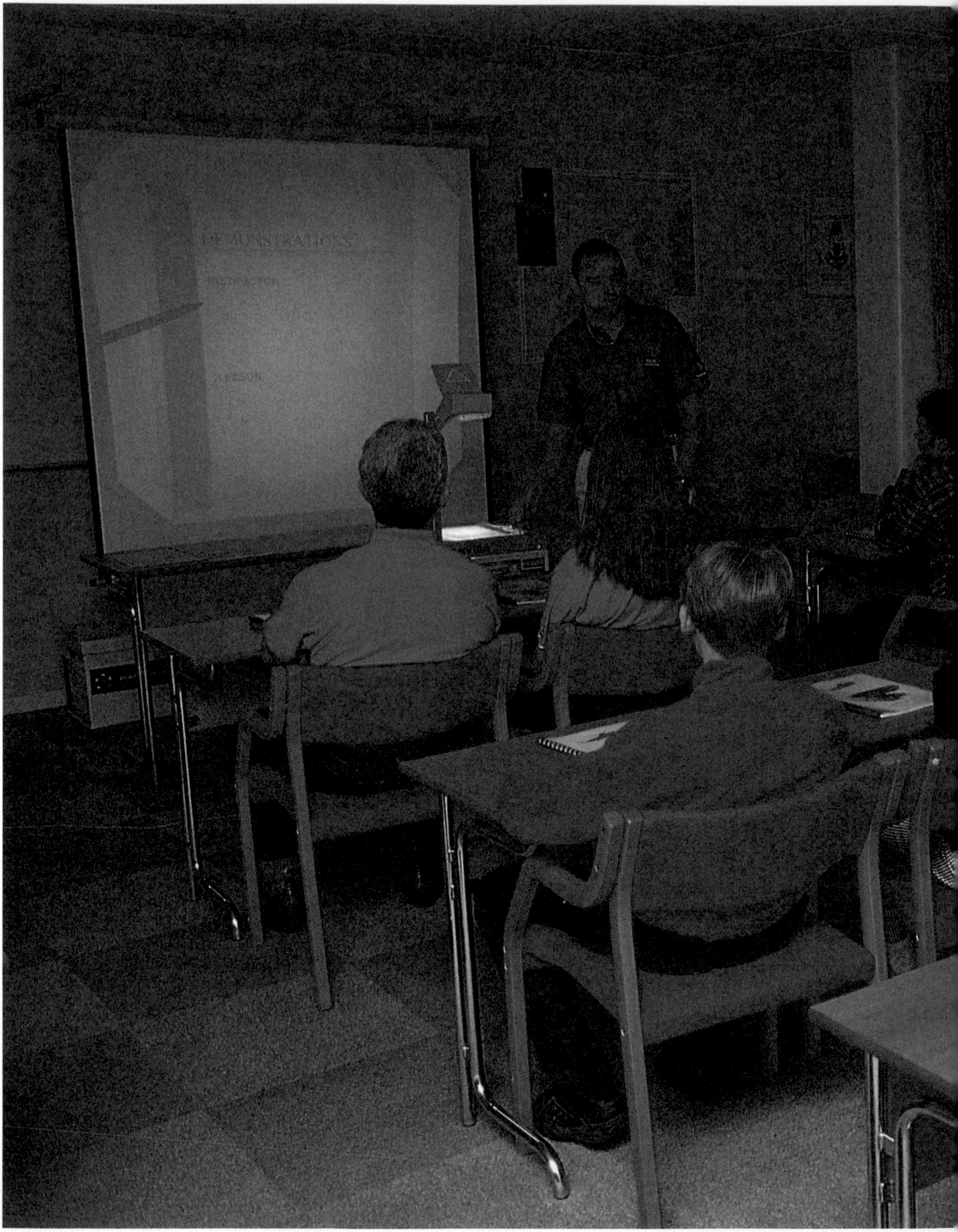

Classroom Teaching

Classroom Teaching

In diver training, knowledge and understanding of theory is a necessary part of even the most basic qualification. In formal education, most teaching takes place in the classroom, in diver education there are a number of ways in which theoretical knowledge can be presented.

Employing techniques such as discussions, tutorials, lessons, and practical demonstrations, or a combination of some or all, are important alternatives to the formal classroom situation. However, the use of a classroom or dedicated teaching area does encourage learning and can also help to reduce distractions. A modern well equipped classroom with chalkboards, tables, chairs, and projection equipment for visual aids to be presented more effectively, can improve the instructors' presentation and confidence.

This section covers the essential points associated with giving an effective classroom lesson, although it must be emphasized that many of the points made are equally effective in a number of different teaching conditions. It emphasizes the importance of maximizing the visual impact when giving a lesson, and deals with the practical aspects of planning and managing a lesson. This section also highlights the value of preserving valuable pool-time by using the classroom for dry-runs of practical skills, where appropriate.

Preparing the classroom

Whether you are using formal or improvised facilities, try to arrive before your students. An early arrival is particularly useful if you are feeling nervous at the prospect of standing in front of your class. A short settling-in period helps you to relax and allows you to familiarize yourself with the surroundings. This period also gives you an opportunity to check and arrange the facilities to suit your lesson requirements or individual style.

If you are using a chalkboard or dry wipeboard, check the availability of writing utensils and board cleaner. The board should be cleaned to remove any information which may have been left by a previous presenter. If you require the room to be darkened, check the operation of the blinds or curtains and familiarize yourself with the location of light switches. If you are using a slide projector or an overhead projector, make sure they are working correctly. Check that they are correctly aligned with the screen and that the projected image is in sharp focus. Some OHP's carry a spare bulb inside their casing, sometimes these have been used and not replaced! You will also need to locate and check the power supply; it is never safe to assume that a plug socket will be located near to the area where you are going to conduct your lesson.

Figure 27 A modern well equipped classroom does encourage learning.

For this reason it is a good idea to bring along an extension lead. Using your own equipment removes some of the worry and uncertainty from your presentation.

Instructor and student positioning

Before your students arrive, consider where you are going to position yourself, and your class, in order to achieve maximum attention and effectiveness. Remember that accepting an existing classroom format may prove distracting for both you and your students. The most obvious position for the instructor is at the front of the class so that the students' attention is focused on you. However, there are a number alternative formats which can be employed, depending on student numbers. You may consider moving the seating around so that they are positioned where they can best see and hear you clearly. Some people seem to have an aversion to sitting at the front of a class while others avoid sitting close to people they do not know.

Reducing some of the spare seating will discourage the students from spreading themselves around the classroom, and bring them closer to you. Before your lesson begins, check the students seating arrangements from a number of different positions. Make sure that each student has an uninterrupted view of you and your visual aids.

Remember that staggering the seating gives those behind a better view. See fig 28. The position of a projector screen or free standing display board should be checked to ensure that everyone can see without having to move their position.

For practical classroom demonstrations, such as life-saving techniques and lessons involving class participation, you may wish to arrange the seating so that students are positioned around a central area of floor or table. Positioning the class in a circle is an excellent format for discussions as it can encourage an interchange of ideas in an informal and relaxed setting. For tutorials, small groups of tables and chairs can be arranged, preferably placed some distance away from other groups to avoid one group distracting another.

Often classrooms follow the traditional style with a table positioned between the students and presenter. In some classrooms the table and area in front of the chalkboard are raised on a podium giving the presenter a greater field of vision. Take care not to place a physical barrier between yourself and your students as this can also cause a psychological barrier to be formed. See fig 29. This may also discourage them from participating or from feeling part of your presentation.

Figure 28 Stagger the seating so that everyone can see you and your visual aids clearly.

Figure 29 Table acting as a barrier between the instructor and the class.

However, you will need somewhere to place your notes and materials, this can still be achieved if the table is placed or angled a little to one side of where you intend to stand, and not directly between you and your students.

Distractions

No matter how dynamic your presentation or interesting the subject, your students' attention can be distracted in many different ways. The senses we use to learn can be hijacked by the following:

Visual distractions

The most powerful distractions are visual. Anything on display such as wallcharts or posters positioned behind you or within the normal field of vision of the students should be removed or covered up. When using your own visual aids, keep them out of sight until they are required.

Do not leave visual aids on display, when they are no longer relevant to your presentation. Remember to check the size and readability of your visual aids from the back of the class. If they are too small, or if the room is poorly illuminated, they may be difficult to read. Try to position the class so that it is not easy for them to look out of the windows. Remember, one of the major visual distractions can be you, the presenter. Make sure that your mannerisms or appearance do not become the focus of their attention.

Noise

People talking during a presentation can prove distracting and irritating to others, they should be asked politely

Figure 30 Students arranged for an informal tutorial.

to stop until the lesson has finished. Outside noise is usually more difficult to control, although closing any open windows or doors may help to reduce the noise level. If there is a deafening or penetrating noise during your presentation, such as an aircraft flying overhead, rather than trying to shout above the noise, it is best to stop talking until the noise has receded or been removed.

Classroom comfort

The room needs to be comfortable and well ventilated. The room temperature should be warm – too hot and people will become sleepy and restless – too cold, and they will become preoccupied with trying to keep warm. In these extremes of temperature the attention of your class will be focused on their discomfort and not on your presentation. Unless cushioned seating is available, sitting for long periods on hard wooden or plastic chairs can prove uncomfortable. In these situations it may prove beneficial to call a short break to allow people to stretch their legs and / or use the restroom facilities.

Large group presentations

In some respects presentations to large groups are easier than dealing with half a dozen people in a small room. There are potential problems but many are removed as the size of the venue will dictate, to a certain extent, the choice of visual aid to be used. Large halls and lecture theatres lend themselves to the use of slides, film, video projection and overhead projectors.

Slides

If you are using slides try to have them mounted in glass mounts to avoid the loss of focus which sometimes occurs as the slide heats up and distorts, the slides themselves must be pin sharp because any areas slightly out of focus will be very obvious once blown up on a wide screen.

Film

Film usually presents few problems unless it is 'home movie' quality, 16mm professional film projects very well. Slide and film projectors should be as far away from the screen as possible and 'long throw' lenses should be used to ensure good presentation on the screen. It is also essential to have an assistant close to the projector to help with slide jams, film breaks and so on.

Whether you use an infra-red or other wireless control to operate the slide projector will depend on equipment availability, but remember to ensure an uninterrupted path between the infra-red transmitter and the receiver.

Video

Video may be used with a video projector but care should be taken to ensure that the video is as near 'broadcast quality' as possible, otherwise there could be a great drop in quality when projected. 'Hi-8 and Super VHS' should be the minimum standard for home produced video to reduce the loss of quality.

Overhead projector

Care is required in the use of an overhead projector to avoid the 'keystone effect' produced when the projector is too near a vertical screen which is set high to enable everyone to see it.

Figure 31 Delivering a formal lecture.

Figure 32 Remove visual distractions from the students' view.

The lecture

Traditionally the lecture has been looked upon as the most common approach to instruction although it is probably the least efficient method of communicating information, and is of very little use when it comes to communicating skills. Its main weakness lies in the fact that in a lecture the audience are for the most part passive recipients of the facts that the lecturer is putting forward and it is not easy for a lecturer to establish a truly personal relationship with members of the audience. Despite these limitations the formal lecture can, if properly presented, play a useful part in instruction.

The major advantage of lecturing is that it does permit one person to handle a large audience, numbers of one hundred or more at a time, and that once prepared, a good lecture can be used time and time again. An expert, whose time is at a premium, can be used economically in this way. Because the audience are for the most part passive, it is essential that the lecturer prepares the material and the presentation well. The arguments or facts must be developed logically and in a way that the audience can follow because the lecturer has no way of checking that they have been understood. It is important to make full use of visual aids and changes of approach to keep the audience interested.

In the lecture, the way the voice is used is of particular importance, as a continuous monotone soon puts an audience peacefully to sleep. Where possible a lecture may be enlivened by breaking it into shorter stages and interspersing these with brief question periods.

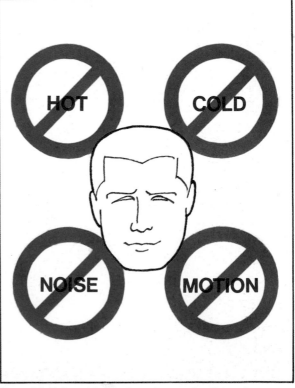

Figure 33 Noise, vision and comfort can be distracting.

The large number of people who can be addressed at one time by this the formal lecture makes it worthwhile and economical to spend extra time and effort on the preparation. To be of the greatest value the lecture needs to be supported by directed reading, discussions in smaller groups and if possible, tutorials.

The lesson

The lesson is the name given to teaching when class numbers vary between ten and twenty. The smaller group allows much more personal contact than is possible in the lecture and permits individual attention when the class is engaged in practical work or in working examples.

The lesson gives the opportunity for considerable class participation through questioning, handling apparatus and practical exercises and is characterized by the interplay that is possible between the instructor and the students. This close contact allows you to judge how well the class is able to understand the material you are presenting to them and gives you the opportunity to change your pace of presentation to suit their rate of assimilation. Where necessary, a difficult point can be repeated or re-explained in a different way. To make the most of this situation you need to acquire the art of oral questioning to check the progress of your students, or to guide them to discover new relationships for themselves.

Figure 34 A less formal approach to traditional methods.

The discussion

Discussion in groups makes an interesting break between periods of more formal instruction. This technique is most effective when the topic chosen is controversial or has aspects on which differing opinions can be expressed. Discussion is of little value in the presentation of factual information, although the expression of opinions will bring out more useful facts. Groups should not be too large, 25 is about the maximum, and there should be a leader or an elected Chairperson.

An informal atmosphere is essential to encourage people to make a contribution and the task of the leader is to keep the comments on the main theme, to keep ideas flowing and to add information if necessary. The leader can initiate the discussion by a brief survey of the topic and an indication of some aspects worthy of consideration, and then directing a question to one of the group. This must be a question that needs a statement of opinion and not a straight 'yes' or 'no' answer or the discussion will terminate there and then.

The leader must tactfully control the contributions and ensure that one or two individuals do not dominate the discussion. The leader must also see that alternative points of view are expressed and can, if necessary, initiate these from their own experience of the topic but must guard against emphasizing their own point of view. Discussion needs careful preparation and the leader must personally have surveyed the topic and have to hand leading questions to use if contributions flag. If members of the group put questions to the leader, these can be used to advantage by turning them back to the group for their comments. It is essential that members are stopped from cross-talking between themselves, and the leader must insist that comments and questions are passed through the chair. Although discussion is unlikely to reach any concrete conclusion, the leader must be prepared to summarize fairly the opinions expressed at its conclusion.

The open forum

In an open forum a number of experts answer questions put to them by an audience. As with discussion, this is perhaps most useful when the questions are on topics that allow the experts to express differing points of view based upon their own experiences. The forum can however, also serve a useful purpose during a lesson by requiring factual answers. A chairperson is essential to ensure that questions are taken across the audience and also to ensure that members of the answering panel do not go on for too long or ride their particular hobby horses.

Questions are not always forthcoming at an open meeting as individuals are sometimes too shy to start the ball rolling and fear that the answers to their questions will be too obvious. It may be a good idea to ask that questions be given to the chairperson, in writing, before the forum starts. This allows one or two questions to be planted if the response is poor, or if full value is not being made of the available expertise. Similarly, one or two members of the audience can be primed with initial questions to get the session under way.

The practical demonstration

Any teaching that involves an element of 'doing' requires the instructor to be efficient at demonstrating. This aspect of presentation is so important that it warrants a section to itself and is considered under the heading *Teaching Basic Skills.* See page 70.

Whilst planning and preparation lay a sound foundation for a lesson or a lecture and will help develop confidence in your ability to handle the subject, the final success of your teaching will depend a lot upon your personality and the way in which you, as a person, are able to communicate with your audience. There are no hard and fast rules which, if followed, will ensure success, but there are a number of important points that can help to give an improved presentation.

The instructor should arrive in the classroom in good time. This allows you to make last minute checks that everything you need is readily available, that the seating is conveniently arranged and also allows you to collect your thoughts before starting. Your presence in the room as the class begins to arrive creates an atmosphere of efficiency and a desire to get down to the task in hand. If you are meeting the class for the first time you should introduce yourself and then state clearly the nature of your subject. Enthusiasm is infectious and it is essential that this enthusiasm comes over through the voice. A bored and listless instructor never captured an audience.

Fig 35 An informal discussion can take place almost anywhere.

Figure 36 Open forums give the audience an opportunity to be involved and to ask questions from the 'experts'.

EXIT

Advanced Lecturing

Advanced Lecturing

All the planning and preparation that has been done beforehand has to be put into practice on the day. No matter how carefully this planning has been thought out, it is important to arrive at the venue early in order to confirm that any required facilities will work in the way that you have planned

The first priority after arrival is to ensure that all the required facilities actually work. Does the Overhead Projector work?, Does the board need cleaning?. What table space is available? Is the extension lead that you brought long enough?

Having ascertained that the necessary facilities are available and working, the next priority is to decide on the layout. The venue may well dictate what flexibility you have to arrange the facilities the way that you want them. While you will have planned the ideal layout beforehand, you still need to confirm that this can be achieved. If not, a compromise will have to be determined which may require some adjustments to the stage managing of your lesson.

Start by familiarizing yourself with the basic facilities of the venue, such as the location of light switches and electric power points, possible locations for projectors, OHPs, flipcharts etc., how blinds or curtains are operated and whether screens or whiteboards are fixed or adjustable.

Figure 37 A handheld microphone should be kept close to the presenter's mouth.

Set up the seating for the class to suit the facilities you intend to use. With the facilities set up to suit your intentions, do not assume that these will automatically work. Some simple checks still need to be made to avoid common pitfalls.

Sit in a number of the seats provided for the class to ensure that all the appropriate facilities are visible from a seated position. It is surprising just how much more of an obstruction the head of an OHP can be to someone who is seated than to someone standing at the same position. Simple repositioning of some seating may avoid this.

Reflections on shiny whiteboards from lights or windows may also not be apparent except when seated, requiring adjustment to lighting or blinds. Note also the sightlines from the front extremities of the class to the visual aids so that you can determine where to position yourself so that you also avoid becoming an obstruction. Having determined the layout, your visual aids need to be fully prepared for use before you start the lesson. The management of their use warrants serious thought and should cover the following:

● *Where will the visual aids be positioned until they are needed?*
(They will need to be out of sight of the class but close to hand. Bulky items such as pieces of equipment which are too large to place entirely out of view will need to be covered).

● *Are they fully prepared and ready for use?*
(They will need to be checked to ensure that they are all present, the right way up and in their correct order. Where needed, fixing materials such as Blu-tac should already be in place).

● *Exactly where will the visual aids be placed or how will they be used during the lecture?*
What layout will be needed on the whiteboard to ensure that all the aids will fit in a logical sequence when needed?
Will you need a table placed nearby on which to display items of equipment at a height sufficient for all the class to see them?
Where will you need to position yourself to use them without blocking the class' view?

● *When will you finish with the visual aids?*
(Some will be used alone and then need to be removed). Where will they be stored after use?. This will need to be somewhere different to those aids still to be used, so as not to disrupt their access. Some visual aids will need to be used for a period of time in conjunction with others. The logistical management of this will need to be preplanned so that one does not obstruct another in terms of either accessibility or the class' view.

Once you have arranged everything to your satisfaction the final check is to have a dry-run through any critical elements to ensure that they will actually work in practice. If the venue is new to you, you will need to familiarize yourself with any lighting or projector controls.

If you are using 35mm slides, a quick run through to ensure that they are all the right way round and the right way up is vital!. Even with less sophisticated aids, such as flashcards, it is worthwhile checking, for instance, that the planned layout will really fit on the size of whiteboard available. It is far better to discover such problems before commencing the lesson, than during the course of the lesson in front of a class!

Using a Microphone

The use of audio aids such as a microphone needs as much forethought as the use of visual aids. Those used in the lecture or presentation situation generally fall into three main types fixed, hand-held, cordless or lapel microphones. All have certain common characteristics, but each has its own individual considerations when in use.

Microphones for lecture/presentation use are generally designed to pick up sound from a direction roughly along an axis directly in front.

While individual design characteristics vary in detail, microphones are much less sensitive to sound from other directions in order to avoid picking up ambient noise which would detract from the clarity of the presenter's voice. For similar reasons, microphones also generally have a set minimum threshold level of sound. Sounds of a lower level will not be detected. This is to avoid distracting sounds from directly behind the presenter, being picked up.

These characteristics must be borne in mind when you use a microphone. The presenter's voice must at all times be directed towards the microphone along its axis. The microphone must also be kept fairly close to the presenter's mouth, at a reasonably constant distance. See fig 37.

Turning the head away from the microphone to point to something on a screen behind or to one side of the presenter will result in an abrupt reduction in volume.

Similarly, if the presenter moves back from the microphone there will be a reduction in volume as the sound of the presenter's voice reaching the microphone falls to the threshold level and is cut off. Movement towards or away from the microphone will, in any case, result in annoying variations in volume even if the sound reaching the microphone remains above the threshold level.

Figure 38 lapel or cordless microphones are easy to use.

Figure 39 Check for obstructions – OHP arm.

Lapel microphones are easier to use than the fixed type due to the constant relationship between the microphone and the presenter. Hand held microphones require a conscious effort on the part of the presenter to maintain the microphone in the appropriate position at a time when concentration is likely to be fully committed to the presentation itself. Fixed microphones require a conscious effort to avoid the above problems but do leave the presenter's hands free to deal with lesson notes etc. Handle notes carefully since, being nearer to the microphone than the presenter, they could well provide a source of distracting noise.

The position of the loud speakers also warrants consideration. If too much sound from the speakers is picked up by the microphone an annoying screeching sound, called 'feedback', is produced. Avoid this by careful positioning of the speakers relative to the microphone and adjustment of the system volume. Fixed microphones can be positioned to avoid this problem but when mobile microphones are used (either hand held or lapel) the presenters must be very careful where they move in relation to the speakers if their movements are not to be accompanied by distracting 'feedback'.

Depending on the position and orientation of the audience relative to the presenter, it may be almost impossible for the presenter to hear the sounds that the audience will hear. The overall volume of the system will therefore have to be set very carefully beforehand, with some allowance for the different characteristics of the room when full of people. Alternatively, the system will need to be monitored and adjusted as necessary by a separate operator situated where they can properly monitor the sound reaching the audience. This is by far the best solution as the operator can also make volume adjustments to avoid 'feedback' should the need arise.

Formal lectures

Formal lectures are in essence no different from any other classroom teaching situation. The aspects to be considered are much the same although the scale and scope of some of them may be quite different.

Formal lectures are usually given where the number of students involved is relatively large, as is frequently the case for instance on skill development courses. The number of students involved will require a relatively large classroom and this will have further effects which will need to be taken into account when planning the format of the lesson. This will need to be considered right at the outset of planning the lecture as, by their very nature, such venues will frequently provide less flexibility for adaptation on the day.

The larger the group becomes the more consideration needs to be given to where the instructor will be positioned relative to both the students and the visual aids. The greater the number of students, the greater the potential for the instructor to block the students' view of the visual aids. Similarly, if you have not properly thought it through beforehand, the logistics of handling the visual aids can also become a distraction.

These considerations have been addressed in the beginning of this section.

Larger groups also mean that some students will be further away from the instructor and visual aids. This requires you to speak louder to ensure that your voice will carry, and to prepare your visual aids so that they are of sufficient size and contrast to be readable from the rear of the class.

The reduced flexibility of formal lectures will also have an impact on how you deliver the lesson. With small groups, class involvement is much easier and more controllable. Posing questions to a large class needs more specific targeting, if one or two members are not to dominate the responses.

Where practical aspects are involved, e.g. practice in using decompression tables or navigational charts, a completely different approach will need to be planned. Effective instruction of such aspects will be impossible with a large group. Such lessons will need to be divided into those aspects that can be adequately covered in a formal lecture to a large group – such as the basic principles and procedures – and then a separate session planned with the class broken into smaller groups, each with a supervising instructor, for the practical aspects. The aspects to be covered in the group session will need to be planned by the instructor giving the formal lecture as they need to be considered as an extension of the formal lecture, not separate lessons. Each of the assisting instructors will need to be suitably briefed to ensure that all the groups receive instruction which is consistent and covers the content intended by the lecturer.

Conference presentations

Conference presentations are essentially the extreme version of the formal lecture. The size of the audience is much larger and the circumstances under which the presentation will be delivered offer little flexibility. Preparation and planning must therefore allow for this. These are high profile events and it goes without saying that presentations must be of the highest quality. This requires thorough planning and preparation based on as much knowledge as can be gained in advance of the venue, its facilities and the event organization.

Prior to the event the organizers should provide details of the visual aid facilities available at the venue. Often this includes guidance on the physical size of the auditorium and the screens onto which images are projected. As the facilities will be managed by conference staff, it is essential that visual aids conform to the organizer's specification and are properly labelled for ownership, orientation and sequence. Failure to do so dramatically increases the likelihood of problems during the presentation.

Conferences are, by their nature, run to a very specific timetable. In order to ensure that this is achieved each session will need to be managed by a Chairperson. They are responsible for not only ensuring adherence to the timetable, but also for introducing the various presenters to the audience and for managing any question and answer sessions which may follow the presenters conference presentation.

Figure 40 View from the podium at a large conference.

A short biosketch should be prepared prior to the event and should be submitted to the organizers for the session Chairperson's use when introducing you.

It is essential that presentations are very tightly tailored to the time allotted by the organizer. Indicator lights may be positioned where they can be seen by the presenter (not by the audience) and controlled by the session Chairperson. These normally indicate when there is a short time left to run (e.g. 2 min) and when the presenter should consider finishing.

Presentations should be well rehearsed to ensure that they conform to the time allotted. Some presenters prefer to read from a script to make sure they run to time. This script must be carefully prepared if it is not to make the presentation stilted and awkward. Lines of closely spaced typing are very difficult to read in a relaxed manner. Prepare your script using a larger than normal typeface and format it into short, well spaced paragraphs. This format enables the wording to be followed more easily. Should it be necessary to look up from the script, to refer to a visual aid for example, it is much easier and quicker to re-find the place in the script again.

Some presenters prefer to use 'key word' notes. While this aids a more conversational style of presentation and can overcome the stilted delivery associated with scripts, it introduces additional considerations, particularly in regard to timing, as this will be less precise. Timing guides embedded as stage directions at intervals in the notes can assist in keeping the presentation to time, but need practice in their use beforehand.

The size of the audience can at first seem quite daunting. Because of this size the presenters usually stand on some form of stage or rostrum. This has the effect of increasing the distance between the presenter and the audience. Illumination is generally directed at the presenter while the house lights over the audience are turned down – this makes it very difficult for the presenter to see the audience. The sum of these effects is to depersonalise the audience and to make them feel much more remote from the presenter. The reality of the situation is thus much less daunting than might be expected.

Questions following the presentation can either be taken immediately after the presentation or deferred to an 'open forum' at the end of the session. The Chairperson will dictate which will be the case and this will depend upon how they need to adjust the overall session timing. Irrespective of when questions are taken, the Chairperson will still dictate which member of the audience will ask the question and, in the case of an 'open forum', who is to answer. This is essential as the sound engineer will only make 'live' any microphone that is being spoken into. All others are kept 'dead' to avoid interference and extraneous noise.

Following the presentation, the organizer will normally request a full transcript of your presentation for publishing in the Conference Proceedings. This does not normally include all visual aid material, as many of these are visual back-up for words that will appear in the transcript. Where visual material presents information which is referred to in the transcript but not actually included in it, e.g., diagrams or tabulation etc., these should also be provided with the transcript. Questions and answer sessions are recorded by the Conference sound engineer and a transcription of these will be included by the organizer.

Figure 41 Presenter at a lectern.

Figure 42 Questions following the presentation can either be taken immediately after the presentation or deferred to an 'open forum' at the end of the session.

Visual Aids

Visual Aids

The key to success in presenting an effective lecture or lesson is the ability to capture and hold the audiences attention, and to present the subject in a way that can be easily understood and remembered.

Remember the importance of vision in the learning process, the spoken word alone rarely achieves the desired result. The best way to ensure your message is understood is to use words with good visual support, we give this the generic title ''Visual Aids''. The purpose of this section is to show you how to become a more effective presenter and how to use the different media available to create your own visual aids. We will also show you that it is not difficult to produce presentations of a very high standard, ensuring that your message is heard, seen and more importantly, understood.

This section will consider the various types of visual aids available and the techniques employed in their application.

Models

The first point to remember is that there is no substitute for the real thing! If you are presenting a lesson on, for example, mask, fins and snorkel, then have examples of them with you rather than drawings and photographs. The visual aid in this instance is the actual piece of equipment as it is small enough to be easily handled, but large enough to be seen (provided, of course, that

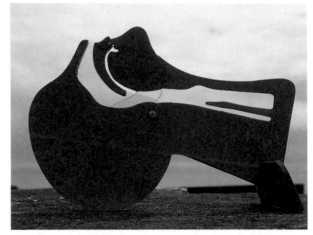

Figure 43 Simple model illustrating good neck extension.

you are not lecturing to a very large number in a large room).

There obviously comes a point where practicality steps in and it may not be possible to have actual examples to hand due to their size. For example, the internal workings of a regulator are too small, complex and difficult to show to a large group. If your objective is to teach

Figure 44 Using a chalkboard properly requires a degree of skill.

Figure 45 Using a Dry wipe board.

the principle, you will probably need to use simplified diagrams or models. Once you have established how it works in principle you can then display the real thing so that the students can identify various features. Some presentations will therefore use a mix of visual aids.

Models require thought and ingenuity to produce, but once made should last for a long time. A model should show only the operating principles and avoid unnecessary detail. Check that the model is functioning correctly just before the presentation. Equipment, the real thing, and good models which demonstrate basic principles, are valuable teaching aids which will hold your students' attention. However, beware of building your presentation around a visual aid or model just because it happens to be available.

Chalkboard – Dry wipe board

Chalkboards may be regarded as the traditional means of displaying information to a class. Included under this category is the dry wipe board which is usually white and is written/drawn on using water based coloured pens. Very often the dry wipe board is also magnetic. See fig 45.

A chalkboard should not be used as an instructors' scribbling pad. It is important to prepare a draft plan of the information to be displayed as part of your lesson notes – notes on the colour and size of heading should also be included. Chalkboards and dry wipe boards are particularly useful for building up a logical sequence of the information being presented, or as a spontaneous and immediate medium for class participation i.e. writing down your students' contributions to the subject. However, to be effective you will need to practice regularly as its use requires a fairly high degree of skill if your presentation is to look tidy and clear.

A board which is black on one side and white on the other, is very useful, doubling as a chalkboard and a projector screen. A clip on the top of the board or a supply of 'Blu-tac' enables it to be used for displaying artwork, photographs or diagrams. The advantages of using this type of board are their simplicity and low cost. However, there are a number of possible disadvantages. Unless you are practiced at producing neat handwriting and your spelling is good, you will need to take care.

When you write on the board you will occasionally turn your back to the class, and you may have a tendency to talk to the board as you write rather than to the class. It is also time consuming in that precious class time may be lost as you physically write information onto the board.

There is no doubt that there is a place for the chalkboard/dry wipe board in our visual aids armoury, but care must be taken in its use otherwise your presentation will be less than professional.

Figure 46 'Blu-tac' secures visual aids to most surfaces.

Figure 47 Flip Charts are versatile for small groups.

Flip charts and posters

A flip chart is simply a collection of pre-prepared diagrams/statements which are collectively held together and displayed by 'flipping' the top one over to reveal the next in the series. The paper needs to be fairly large and the lettering and diagrams bold, neat and easily read. Care should be taken to ensure that the next chart in the series cannot be seen through the one being displayed, and for this reason it is often a good idea to use every other sheet, thereby putting a blank in between each display sheet. Flip charts are readily available from most good stationers. Size A1 is a manageable size to use. However, smaller sizes A2 and A3 can be used on portable displays for classes of 3/4 students. Rolls of light coloured wallpaper and lining paper are ideal for this purpose, and felt tipped pens make perfect markers for this system.

A sequence of posters and pictures not only acts as a good visual communication for your students, but can also serve as an aid to your lesson progression and order by reminding you of the points you need to cover or emphasize.

Flash cards

In their simplest form, flash cards are pieces of either paper or card carrying key words which are then fixed to a wall or other display board.

They are very effective as visual aids but great care is needed in their preparation and use, particularly in how the cards are displayed.

Firstly, it is essential that they stay in place, and secondly that they are arranged in an orderly fashion on the display board to avoid a confused jumble. They may be held in place by pins, magnets, 'Blu-tac' or even with 'Velcro' type material on a flannel board.

Note: 'Blu-Tac' or 'Buddies' are a putty-like material with adhesive properties and can be used for short term or long term display purposes, but use on dusty surfaces should be avoided.

If the choice is 'Blu-tac' or 'Buddies' remember to soften and warm the material before use otherwise it will not stick! One or more pea-size pieces should be applied to the back of the card or item to be displayed before beginning your lesson, so that, at the appropriate time, you can simply pick up the card and press it firmly onto the display surface. The main advantage with cards prepared in this way is their ability to be used on any clean surface i.e. a wall, side of a filing cabinet or even a door.

One problem common to both the flip chart and flash card is the production of the text. If your handwriting and artistic capabilities are poor then it could well be worth investing in a set of stencils, but do remember to fill in the gaps in the letters after the stencil has been removed! Make the text large enough to be seen by the students at the back of the class and try to use colour where possible. For an average size class of up to, say, 15 then the text needs to be of the order of 7.5 cms (3 inches) in height. The use of colour and different styles of lettering is discussed later in this section.

Figure 48 Simple stencilling for neat lettering.

Figure 49 Flash cards carrying your key words.

Overhead projector (OHP)

This device is becoming ever more common and is rapidly becoming the 'norm' for any form of presentation, be it to a large or a small group.

The projector throws an image from a flat horizontal bed onto a screen behind the presenter. The projected image results from a transparency or 'viewfoil' which the presenter places on the projector in the required sequence. The transparencies are usually A4 size and are prepared by hand, using a photocopier to copy printed images, or using computer software programs designed specifically for this use, upon which is written/drawn text or diagrams. Colour can be incorporated into the design by applying coloured acetate or by using a colour printer with your computer. Viewfoils can be used for straight text and are readily suited to the use of the 'reveal' technique''. That is, the information is covered completely and revealed only when you wish it to be revealed. Complex viewfoils can be built up using a series of overlays. See fig 52 on page 60.

While the OHP is a very powerful tool the presenter has to be very careful in its use. First and foremost you should not try to present too much information on each viewfoil. The amount of information presented may be controlled to a certain extent by the size of the text, which should be about 36 point for headings and 24 point for the rest of the text. Key words and phrases should be presented as 'Bullet Points' in much the same way as you would use 'Flash Cards'.

If you wish to include diagrams the[r] simplified schematic types rather tha[n] [draw]ings. It is also possible to have 35mm sli[de] on to OHP viewfoils.

With any presentation it is important to position yourself so that you do not block the class' view of the screen. Plan your position relative to the screen, the class and the projector.

Overhead projectors are designed to display images on a screen positioned overhead and angled, in practice this is rarely the case as mobile screens are more flexible in their use. Usually screens are positioned vertically behind the projector arm, and as a general rule the screen needs to be as high as possible, but that in itself is a drawback in that this produces a 'keystone effect', to counteract this the screen should be angled forward at the top. The size of the screen dictates the size of your audience; refer to the dimensions in the diagram. See fig 50.

A major distraction can be the machine itself, what do you do while changing the viewfoils? Do you switch it off or leave it on? To start with, it is better to switch off between viewfoils, but as you gain experience it is possible to change viewfoils without producing a white screen between them by covering the platen with a blank sheet of paper before you remove/apply viewfoils.

Remember, continually switching the OHP off and on can cause the bulb to blow. The OHP appears simple to operate, but requires a good deal of practice if you are to utilise its enormous potential as a teaching aid.

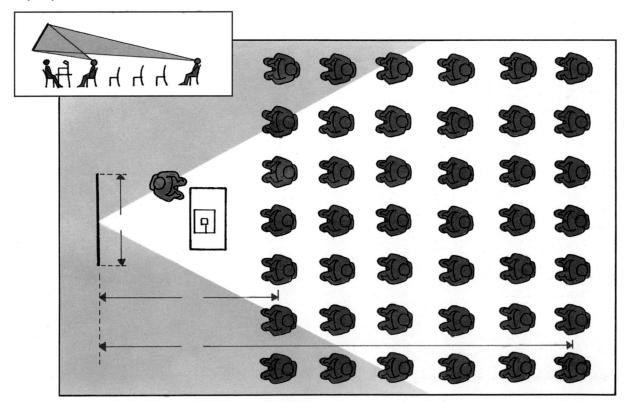

Figure 50 The size of the screen dictates the size of your audience.

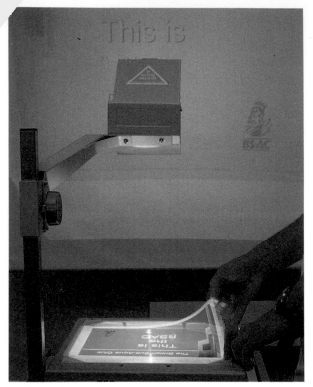

Figure 51 The Overhead Projector (OHP).

Flannel boards and magnetic boards

These are boards which allow diagrams and flash cards to be firmly fastened in place. The flannel board is merely a board covered in flannel or brushed nylon (or for improvisation a blanket) to which the hooks on the 'Velcro' type fasteners will attach.

Visual aids are attached to magnetic boards using small magnets or magnetic strips attached to the back of the item to be displayed.

The above types of visual aid are relatively simple to make and cheap but they do have limitations, not the least in the size of class you are capable of handling. You would not, for example, be able to use any of the above very effectively if you were talking to a very large audience in a theatre.

Slide projector

The slide projector lends itself to large theatre style presentations where a very large image is required.

One obvious advantage of the slide is that photographs of all types of equipment, situations and techniques may be used. The most popular format is 35mm film, giving a 24mm x 36mm original. This has the advantage of being compact, portable, and standardised yet gives a high quality image. But apart from photographs, slides can also be prepared of text matter, either by photographing prepared sheets, or using a computer presentation program. Remember, the comments made previously about the amount of information/text displayed also applies to the slide, keep it simple!

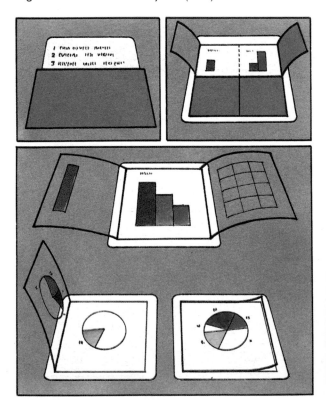

Figure 52 Overlay techniques for the Overhead Projector.

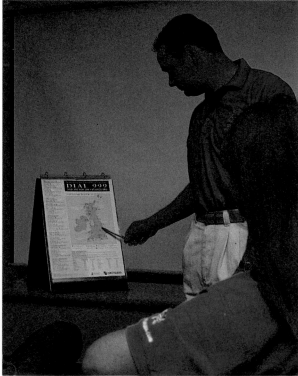

Figure 53 Folding display board for small groups.

Computers

Personal computers are an excellent means of producing visual aids, particularly 35mm slides and OHP transparencies. A number of specialised software programs are available for this purpose which offer an excellent quality of presentation combined with reasonable ease of use. Some major examples are 'Microsoft Power Point' and 'Harvard Graphics' but many other graphic PC programs offer the possibility. The computer files can be transferred directly into slides by a computer bureau, or you can photograph the PC screen to produce an acceptable result at less cost. This is relatively simple and all you require is a camera loaded with 100 ASA slide film, a lens with a focal length in excess of 135mm (a 70–200mm zoom lens is ideal) and a darkened room to ensure correct exposure.

The camera should be placed as far from the screen as possible to ensure that the individual pixels on the screen merge together in the final photograph, too near and the lettering will be seen as a group of dots with no smooth edges. Exposures should be bracketed and good results will require some experimentation. An exposure of f8 for half a second should be used as the start point.

Fonts, size and colour

The correct choice of font or typeface will make your presentations clearer, easier to read, and therefore, help to convey your message more effectively. Some typefaces lend themselves to use in presentations but others should be used with caution, if at all.

Figure 55 Slide projector and stand.

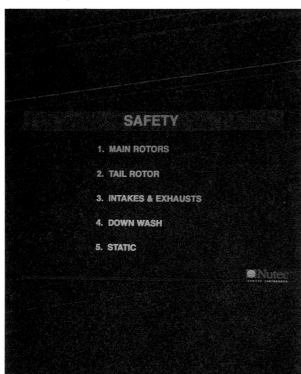

Figure 54 Computer generated slides.

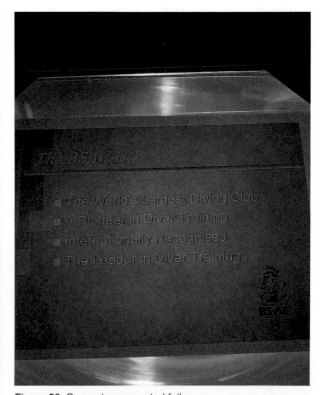

Figure 56 Computer generated foils.

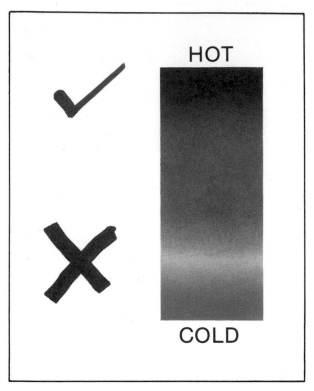

Figure 57 Using colour for emphasis.

Sans-serif fonts such as Helvetica, Swiss, Arial or Univers are best suited to presentations as they are easier to read when viewed from a distance. 'Sans' is the French word meaning 'without'; making sans-serif fonts those without additional strokes.

Times is the best known of serif fonts. Serif fonts are better for densely packed body-text sizes such as reports, books etc., they are considered easier to read as the serif help guide the eye from letter to letter. This style of font should be used for your handouts. Decorative fonts should be avoided as they can be difficult to read.

When you prepare a presentation, try to avoid using more than two different fonts in your display, for emphasis use bold, italics or underline. Decide before you start on the fonts, styles and sizes you intend to use for your titles, subtitles, bullets and so on, and then use them consistently throughout your presentation.

Take care in the use of UPPER-CASE letters. All text in upper-case may be effective as a heading or title because you are forced to read the text character by character, but if the text is long it becomes tiring to read and the impact is lost.

The use of colour in your presentation can add impact and clarity to your message and may be used to highlight important points, such as Red for things you should not do, and Green for things you can do. Reversing this sequence of colours could make your visual aid confusing as subconsciously we assume that Red is danger and Green is OK. However, use this combination carefully as there are a number of people who are red/green colour blind.

The BSAC is the largest diving club in the world.

The BSAC is the largest diving club in the world.

The BSAC is the largest diving club in the world.

The BSAC is the largest diving club in the world.

The BSAC is the largest diving club in the world.

Figure 58 Avoid using too many different types of fonts in one display as they may prove difficult to read.

The British Sub-Aqua Club

The British Sub-Aqua Club

The British Sub-Aqua Club

The British Sub-Aqua Club

Figure 59 Font sizes 12pt, 18pt, 24pt and 36pt. Light, Italic, Medium and Bold type faces.

The basic rules are (and this applies to all visual aids):

● Keep it simple
● Be consistent
● Choose the correct combination of colours

The first two points are self explanatory but the third needs some explanation. The easiest way to choose a colour combination is to use a colour wheel. See fig 60. The wheel is split into warm and cool colours, and colours opposite each other are said to be 'complementary' to each other.

Cool colours (the blue side of the wheel) are best for backgrounds while the warm colours (reds and oranges) work best for text. A good combination is a blue background with yellow text. Great care should be exercised when choosing colour combinations, for example red text on a blue background may be illegible.

A significant difference between slides and overhead projector viewfoils is that slides tend to work better with darker backgrounds and light text, whereas the converse is true for OHP viewfoils, where light backgrounds and dark text are preferred.

Text charts
Use emphatic headings with strong verbs to grab attention and keep the same tense throughout. Only introduce one idea per chart. Keep the text concise. Use short words and sentences with no more than 6-8 words per point and no more than 6-8 lines per chart.

Film and video
The major advantage of these two media is their ability to employ sound and motion or to show demonstrations of skills, or items of equipment in operation.

These powerful visual aid tools should not be used as a substitute for the instructor, but should be used interactively with the instructor controlling the lesson. The film or video becomes part of the lesson, rather than replacing it. Beware of the temptation to put on a film or video, leave the class to watch and then return at the end to discuss what they have seen and ostensibly check if the pupils have absorbed the information.

A far better approach is for the film or video to be used to illustrate certain points introduced by the instructor, with the opportunity afterwards to ask and answer questions or to discuss points raised.

Take care when using film not to stop and start it too frequently as it is not robust and can break easily. Video is a far better medium, as a cassette can be readily stopped, rewound, slowed down and so on without risk of damage.

Training videos are used widely throughout industry and have already replaced a number of traditional teaching methods. However, it must be remembered that high quality professionally produced video production is still expensive, and can cost up to £1,000 per minute of film to produce. Amateur videos can be useful in showing a particular technique or piece of action, but often suffer from poor editing or composition.

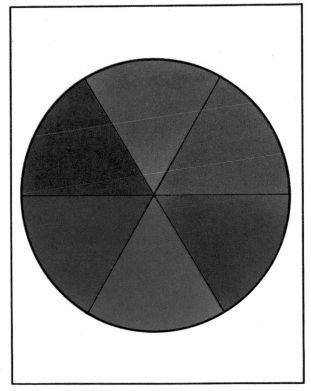

Figure 60 Colour wheel.

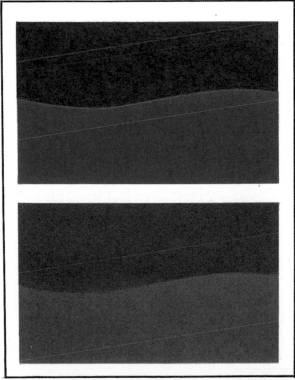

Figure 61 Colour combinations to avoid.

A number of 16mm films are available relating to various aspects of diver training. Where they are completely relevant to the lecture subject they may make an interesting alternative to other forms of presentation. However, you should see the film and be sure that it is relevant and teaches the subject to your satisfaction before it is shown. The content and timing of the film is entirely in the hands of the film maker, and therefore outside your control.

Conditions for projection

Slides and films can only be shown effectively in a blacked out room. If the black-out is inadequate, the projected image will be poor and will have a marked effect on your students' concentration and learning. There is nothing more distracting than having shafts of light across a screen from a window or a badly positioned light or having the room so bright that the images cannot be seen at all. You should be prepared to black-out or cover sources of light (usually windows).

Generally, overhead projectors do not require as dark a room as slides and film. Video presentation may be in the form of a normal TV or a video projector and the type of presentation will affect the light requirement of the room. The important point is to remember to check the room well in advance to ensure that you have the necessary black-out materials available should they be needed.

For films, accurate focussing and correct sound reproduction is equally important.

Computer software

A wide range of software is offered for the purpose of preparing presentations. There is no significant difference in principle between software for preparing either lessons, or presentations, except perhaps the budget available.

The advantage of presentation software is that it has been designed to do exactly what you need to do, and to do this in a well-organized and effective manner. Most programs will also help you through the preparation process and will offer you the facility of producing OHP viewfoils, 35mm slides, printout on paper, a presentation directly on the PC screen or via a computer-controlled projector, as well as lesson notes and handouts. Once you have adopted the habit of using this powerful teaching aid, you will soon find it more than able to meet your needs.

Preparation starts with the decision to use a 'standard' background scheme and layout for your lesson/presentation, or to design something new. The software will offer you a choice of standard layouts, one of which may well suit your needs. Should you decide to design a personal layout, then it can always be used again for other lessons.

Having decided on the design you can then accept or modify the choice and sizes of fonts to be used. Headings will use a larger font, with sub-headings and body matter using smaller sizes. Avoid going too small, usually 2 or 3 levels of emphasis are suitable for most

Figure 62 Using a PC to support your presentation.

Figure 63 Providing it is relevant a video showing the action can introduce an interesting change.

presentations. Consider whether you need to add some other elements to the master layout, such as a club logo, or the lesson title as a footer note, it will then appear automatically on each slide.

A computer screen is·wider than it is high, so this is the format normally offered. You can modify this to a 'portrait' format, but this is inadvisable as it will not fit an on-screen PC presentation, and if you are preparing OHP foils, a landscape format projects better and is better viewed by your audience. Another advantage is to keep all your lessons in a standard format, which makes them easier to handle and to use.

Prepare the content carefully, being sparing yet clear with your words. Do not overcrowd the screen, if necessary sub-divide the topic and go to a further slide. Use graphic illustrations wherever appropriate. Most programs come with a selection of 'clip-art' which can be inserted into suitable positions in your lesson, or you can prepare illustrations using a drawing program or a scanner. Try to avoid lessons which contain only words, they do not make maximum use of the powerful sense of vision.

Preparing OHP slides

Select a format which produces a dark image on a light background, this will project more clearly. If you have a suitable laser or bubblejet printer, then you can print the slides directly onto foil transparencies. If your printer is able to print in colour, then you can also benefit from the use of colour in your presentation. Alternatively, you can print out on plain paper and then use a photocopier to make the foils.

The result in both cases will be a very crisp transparency which will lend authority to your presentation.

Store the original presentation file on your hard disk or a diskette so that you can easily amend one or several slides for any future event.

Preparing a PC presentation

This can take several forms:

● direct presentation on a PC screen, the largest you can find, which is suitable for small groups of up to about 6. Another possibility is to connect several screens so that each screen can support a small group
● feeding a transparent LCD screen which can be laid onto an OHP screen and projected, suitable for medium sized groups where an OHP could be used
● feeding a projector which will produce a large image, effective for the largest size groups.

An advantage of 'live' presentation directly from the PC is that the lesson can be set up to automatically reveal the next slide or heading with a click of the mouse. A selection of 'wipes' and 'dissolves' can be used to add effect, and a degree of animation is possible. Additionally, sound files can be linked to the appearance of a slide or a specific element in the presentation, where appropriate. This also allows a presentation to run automatically following a timed sequence, without the intervention of a presenter.

The above procedure is generally true of well-known software packages such as 'Microsoft Power Point', 'Lotus Freelance Graphics' and 'Harvard Graphics'. These programs are entirely suitable for the preparation of teaching aids for all types of instructional situations. They will become easier and quicker to use as you gain familiarity with the process.

Figure 64 Using Microsoft Powerpoint software to generate 35mm slides or OHP foils.

Figure 65 Using the computer to display your presentation.

Making your own visual aids

For adhesive display systems use coloured art board which is available from artists' supply shops. A wide range of colours are available and the boards can be cut into strips or shapes using a sharp knife or a modeller's scalpel.

For caption cards or labels for key words – use strips of art board of standard size and colour. Use different colour board or ink for headings or points to be stressed.

Cut out the shapes to mimic the object where possible e.g. navigational buoys, boats, etc. These help relate to the real thing. Shapes can be made to fit together like a jigsaw puzzle to achieve the final object shape.

Ready made flip chart pads are available in various sizes from good stationery suppliers, or you can make your own from end of line wall paper rolls or plain lining paper.

Small magnets or strips of flexible magnetic adhesive tape can be obtained from ironmongers, or the seals on dis-used refrigerators can be used to support a mobile visual aid. See fig 67.

Coarse grade sandpaper glued or stapled to the back of your visual aid is adequate for flannel board purposes as long as the object is no heavier than card. To support cards on most surfaces 'Blu-tac' or 'Buddies' are adequate.

Coloured adhesive film is the best way to provide large areas of colour on diagrams or transparencies. Painting in the area with felt tip pens will do, but the density of colour tends to vary and cause a streaky or mottled appearance. Pieces of film can be pre-cut or the film and the surplus trimmed off.

Clear lettering is the secret of good visual aids, whether writing by hand on the board, or key words on cards. Print rather than write, and use a straight edge beneath the words to avoid them running downhill.

A drawing board and T-square are useful aids to ensure that diagrams and wording are parallel and straight: draw feint pencil lines for the top and bottom limits of the lettering. Plot out the length of the words to ensure there is enough space, use more than one strip of card where several words are necessary.

If your printing is good, felt tip pens are ideal for the production of teaching aids. If you cannot print tidily then consider using stencils or 'letraset', which are individual stick on letters – and although expensive, they provide a neat quality finish. Remember the possibility of projecting an image on to a sheet of paper, then drawing it in using chalk or pens. Another useful aid for enlarging a small diagram is a pantograph device expressly designed for this purpose and often sold as a children's toy. These are useful for making rough drafts, which can be easily tidied up as they are completed.

DIY portable visual aid boards

A simple portable board for use when presenting topics to small groups, this board consists of a panel of plywood, matt black on one side for use as a chalkboard, and white on the other for use as a small screen or for

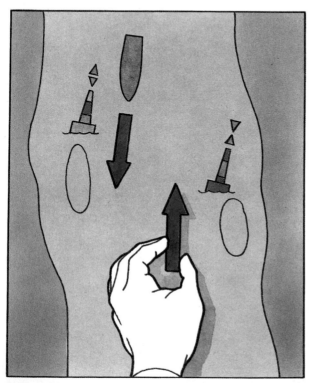

Figure 66 Cardboard cutouts for a lesson on navigation.

Figure 67 Magnetic strip and sandpaper fixed to models.

the application of Blu-tac. The size of the board makes it slightly larger than a standard flip chart pad (70cm x 50cm) so that it can be used for that style of presentation as well.

Construct the board from 10mm plywood, 80cm x 60cm. Face one side either with white laminate or with a white enamelled steel panel taken from a discarded freezer or refrigerator. This will provide you with a magnetic board yet another system for displaying your visual aids!. Paint the other side with several coats of matt black paint. Remember to carefully rub down the surface between coats in order to achieve a smooth surface. The support blocks can be made from any suitable timber, approximately 25mm thick by 6cm-8cm deep by approximately 25cm long. The slightly angled slot should be carefully sawn fractionally wider than the thickness of the board once it has been faced with the steel or laminate. The board will stand in these slots leaning back by approximately 50^0. Use large clips to secure a flip pad to the board when using this system. See fig 70.

Another simple and effective visual aid board which doubles as a diagram storage case comprises two similar sized sheets of plywood (hardboard will do if you want to use it for storage/transport only, rather than as a chalkboard) hinged down one side with a strip of wide (10cm) adhesive tape. A slot can be cut on the opposite side as a hand-hold, and elastic or webbing straps can be used to close it. The four different faces of the boards can be painted matt black or white, or faced with metal or formica to give the versatility of the simple board (as previously described). This system can also be supported in the same way as the metal board – with wooden strips having two slots, or the webbing straps can be slackened slightly so that it stands up, hinge side uppermost.

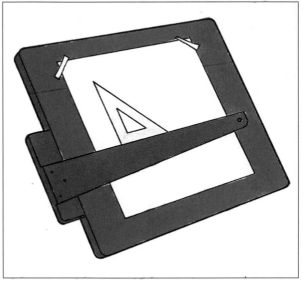

Figure 69 Use of a 'T-Square' and drawing board help to produce neat and tidy lettering.

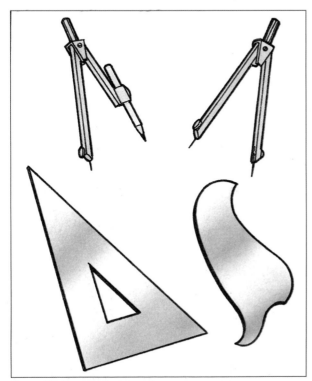

Figure 68 Drawing instruments.

Figure 70 DIY portable display board.

Teaching Basic Skills

Teaching Basic Skills

Training areas

Many of the technical aspects of diver training and most of the introductory work can be taught in the relative comfort and safety of a swimming pool. Sheltered open water may also provide a suitable environment for students to learn their basic skills.

Swimming pools

Swimming pools are generally not designed exclusively for diver training. There are a number of basic requirements which need to be considered before a pool can be judged suitable:

● The water needs to be deep enough to enable underwater skills to be carried out while the student is wholly submerged.

● For students to appreciate the effects of variation of pressure with depth, it is desirable that the pool has a deep section of around 2-3 metres.

● Most training programmes require a good deal of surface activity such as lifesaving and snorkelling practice. Therefore, pools need to be of a reasonable length.

● The shape of a pool is largely immaterial, although, for some aspects of training a completely free shape would be desirable.

Figure 71 Surface dives require sufficient depth.

Figure 72 Diver training in the safety of a swimming pool.

- The slope of the pool-bottom should be gradual and not too steep to allow the students to kneel comfortably. A stepped arrangement of the pool-bottom is preferable.

- Ladders or steps at the deep end are desirable for easy access and exit.

In temperate climates an indoor-pool is preferable to those exposed to the elements. Although, pools can be expensive to hire, they do provide warm and clear water together with changing facilities and other services within easy reach. However, there are a number of drawbacks which are not totally conducive to diver training.

Tiled pools are vulnerable to heavy items of equipment, particularly weight belts, carelessly discarded. Extra care should be exercised by ensuring that lead is plastic coated and cylinders are fitted with protective boots. Replacing broken tiles is an expensive process, and will not endear you to the owners of the pool.

Because of their design, some pools have poor acoustics. Noise generated by air conditioning and water circulation equipment, along with the general hubbub of noise from other water users can make normal conversation difficult.

Overcrowding can impose limitations on the available water space. A pool session may include a number of exercises which necessitate the surface of the pool being used, while others require depth. In this situation activities need to be properly managed and controlled otherwise confusion and personal safety may be at risk. The best solution may be to divide the pool into lanes longitudinally, across the width or even diagonally, using a rope with floats. The roping pattern may have to be changed from time to time to satisfy the changing demands on pool space. A little thought about the best use of pool space before each session will enable you to achieve the best use of the available time.

Open water

Using an open water training area is clearly less expensive than using a swimming pool and allows for more flexibility in terms of availability. Although open water provides a more realistic environment for the student to learn scuba diving, it can, if the water temperature and visibility are not ideal, prove more taxing. These factors could shorten lessons and make class control more difficult. When choosing an open water training area the following should be considered:

- The site chosen should be free from the effects of currents, strong tides and excessive wave action.

Figure 73 Surface lessons using a 'demonstrator'.

Figure 74 Open water training area.

● The static nature of some aspects of training can prove chilling even though the water temperature may be relatively high. Some form of protective clothing is recommended for thermal protection and to protect against abrasions.

● There may be too many natural distractions.

● The training area should have a depth range similar to that of a typical swimming pool, and have easy access and exit points.

● Extra equipment, boats and safety cover may be required.

Choose your open water training area with care. Avoid rocky and uneven areas, and try to find a reasonably flat location where there is enough room to accommodate the size of your class. Sandy areas are ideal, providing there is minimal water movement, even so, you may have to move the class from time to time as sand is easily stirred up, and visibility can deteriorate quickly. Remember, if one of your students gets into difficulties it is likely that you will need to gain access to the shore quickly. Unlike a swimming pool, where the poolside is within easy reach, incidents in open water can become more difficult to deal with if the area chosen is too far from a safe point of exit. Using a Surface Marker Buoy to identify your position underwater and a dive boat as surface cover are wise precautions if training is to be conducted in open areas of sea.

In very cold water and in poor visibility conditions, some aspects of basic training need to be considered with more care. Mask clearing exercises, for example, could prove difficult and risky if the student's face is suddenly exposed to cold water. The exercise becomes more difficult with reduced visibility and the added encumbrance of wearing gloves.

Briefings

Briefing your students before they enter the water is essential if your lesson is to be successful. However, a briefing should be just that – brief! Remember that a poolside is no place for a lecture. Students will only absorb a maximum of four to five items of information prior to a practical lesson, as they are usually preoccupied with the forthcoming event. Therefore, your briefing should be confined to the essentials required for your lesson to work. Although a briefing needs to be brief, it must be complete. You need to ask yourself the following questions:

● What exercise am I going to teach?

● What equipment is required for the exercise?

Figure 75 Typical poolside side briefing – note the back to wall position for the Instructor.

Figure 76 Briefing students prior to an open water dive.

- Where is the exercise going to take place?
- What safety precautions should be taken?
- What signals are going to be used?

Safety

Examine the exercise that you are teaching, and highlight those areas where safety needs to be stressed.

For example, if a Controlled Buoyant Lift is to be taught, then your students must be told to breathe normally during the ascent, and not to hold their breath at any time during the exercise. Alternatively, if the exercise is towing, there is a possibility of colliding with other pool users or the side of the pool. Limit your briefing to those aspects of safety relevant to the exercise, and avoid covering every possible catastrophe that could befall them.

Equipment

Check that your students' equipment is correctly fitted and functioning. Encourage students to check their buddy's equipment, including their pressure gauge. Remember that pre-dive equipment checks should teach the students to identify for themselves the areas of possible problems. Equipment checking should be progressive so that during initial training students become progressively more competent in assembling and fault finding their own equipment, and that of their buddy's.

Exercise

Explain the exercise in principle, and leave the detail to the power of your demonstration. Although students need to know the reason for the exercise, they are unlikely to remember a detailed description of the actions required to perform the exercise.

Discipline

The control of the lesson needs to be established from the start. The position the class are to adopt while in the water, the area of the pool which is going to be used, and where they will be entering and exiting.

Signals

Apart from checking the normal diver to diver signals, there will be additional instructional signals used for the purpose of the lesson. e.g. 'You watch me'. See fig 79 on page 74.

These 5 points can be condensed into the useful mnemonic – S.E.E.D.S.

Use the word SEEDS as an aid-memoire and try to keep your briefings to around 5 minutes duration.

> S – Safety
> E – Equipment
> E – Exercise
> D – Discipline
> S – Signals

Figure 77 Effective visual range for instructing underwater.

Figure 78 Briefing a large group before the lesson.

74

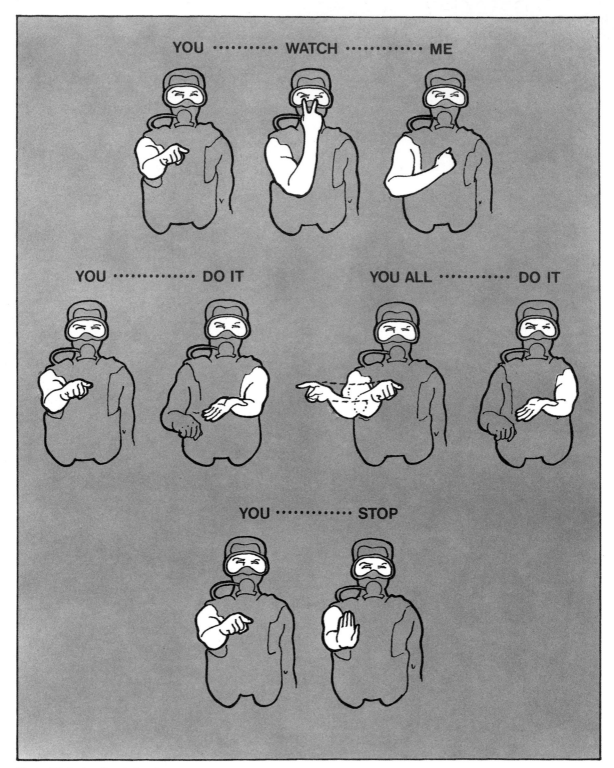

Figure 79 Instructional signals.

Class control

In order to be effective you must gain the undivided attention of your students. Because they want to learn to scuba dive, students will be amenable to a degree of control during lessons. However, you should avoid giving them opportunities to be distracted.

During poolside briefings try to position yourself with your back to a wall so that your students are not distracted by another class or background noise. By keeping your class close together in this way you will be able to speak normally without having to shout to make yourself heard.

If it is necessary to talk to a large group of students on the poolside side, you should collect them together in a tight group – short people at the front, tall people at the back. Make sure that all the class have your attention before giving a briefing, Remember, it is the one who is not listening that may cause you a problem after.

Breakdowns in control usually occur because you failed to plan ahead, or your instructions were ambiguous. For example, if your planned skill lesson required the use of the deep end of the pool, and your instruction to the student was to take their equipment and "place it at the poolside side". This statement gave your students an opportunity to place it anywhere. It would be better to instruct them exactly where to place their equipment. Carefully consider any verbal instructions before giving them. If you instruct a large class to surface-swim two lengths of the pool, then it is possible that some more powerful swimmers will reach and turn on the first length as others are only just arriving. The likely effect is disorder and confusion. It would be better to instruct them all to swim one length and wait until you give the instruction for them to return.

Before entering the pool or training area it is important to consider which is the best and safest area for the skill to be taught? It is safer to teach initial skills in standing depth rather than deep water. Distance swims require access to the length of the pool, while static exercises may use only a corner at the deep end. It may be necessary to access all of these areas during your lesson.

You should plan the use of the available space ahead and confer with any other instructors with regard to their requirements. Think also about an assembly point where your class will meet, kit up, and hold final briefings.

Most instructors find that their students are willing to learn and are co-operative without question. Nevertheless, when students are experiencing a new and foreign environment they like to feel that someone competent is in control. This helps to create a happy and relaxed atmosphere in which training can take place.

Instructor – Student ratio

Class size depends on the activity. With surface skills such as snorkelling or swimming, large groups of 6/8 students can be taught effectively by one instructor, and maybe an assistant to help with demonstrations and corrective instruction. Although larger groups can be taught, it should be remembered that their progress and final quality may be lower, because you cannot give each student the individual attention they may require.

Figure 80 It is better to teach some skills in standing depth and then to progress to shallow and then deeper water.

While individual instruction may be considered ideal, there are disadvantages in a 1:1 ratio. An important part of scuba training is to develop the buddy system, and this is hard to achieve with only one student. The lone student also lacks a sense of competition and finds it difficult to measure their progress against that of their contemporaries. For aqualung instruction, ratios of 2:1 and 4:1 are generally considered to be the most effective numbers. Underwater it is important that you should be able to see all the students without having to turn your head too far from side to side. See fig 81.

Lesson timing
Theory lessons usually have to be completed within a set time, however, practical lessons can sometimes be interrupted to suit the students' progress. Most skill learning is a matter of progression on a continuous basis, and what is not covered in a particular lesson can be carried forward to the next without upsetting the overall scheme. At worst, it means that more practical lessons might be required to cover all the skills adequately. This is seldom a problem in a Branch situation where time is less important, but could prove a problem in a School where the course is of fixed duration.

During practical lesson preparation it may be necessary to time the performance, in the same way as is recommended for theory lesson preparation, but this is only required where time limits apply.

Surface lessons
Many diving skills are taught more easily without the encumbrance of an aqualung – at least in the early

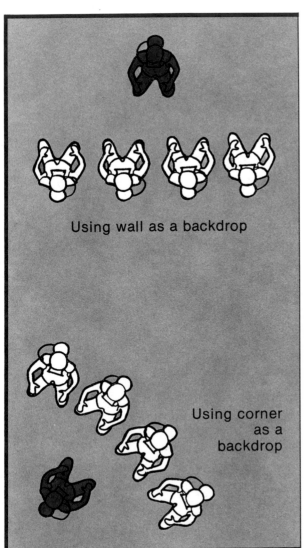

Using wall as a backdrop

Using corner as a backdrop

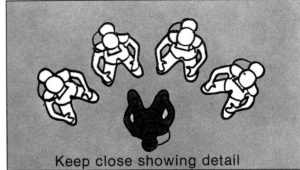

Keep close showing detail

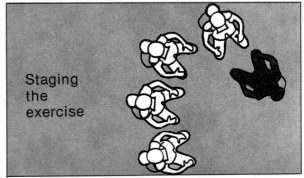

Staging the exercise

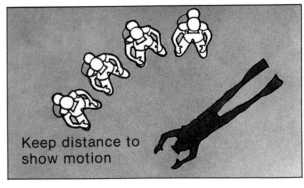

Keep distance to show motion

Figure 81 Class positioning underwater.

stages. For example, finning, use of the snorkel, surface dives, and lifesaving techniques are all skills which can be taught on the surface of the water using basic equipment. Teaching surface skills lends itself to group instruction where more than one instructor can be used. Large numbers of students can be taught by one poolside side instructor using the technique of having an assistant in the water who can demonstrate the various skills and assist in correcting faults.

The importance of good instruction at this level of basic training cannot be over emphasized, since skills learnt at this early stage become the foundation stone for future training, Teaching skills such as finning, mask and snorkel clearing and surface dives requires a great deal of skill on the part of the instructor.

We learnt earlier that each technique needs to be broken down into easy stages, so that the student gains confidence and ability. When analysing any skill it is also important to understand the relationship between a basic skill taught at the beginning of training, and a more complex skill required later. For example, the act of breathing from a snorkel causes the student to inhale and exhale predominantly through the mouth, perfecting this technique now will make breathing from a regulator a familiar routine. Sharing one snorkel between two students while finning also teaches the student breath control and to become used to being without air for a period of time. This exercise may be used as a precursor to sharing a regulator where breath control plays an important part.

Developing a link between a familiar skill and an unfamiliar skill comes with experience and understanding, but this development should always remain relevant to actual diving skills.

Teaching basic skills

Experience has shown that there are many instructional techniques that can be employed when teaching diving skills. The BSAC has always encouraged instructors to develop their own individual styles of teaching, and to avoid a dogmatic approach which says "there is only one way to teach a particular skill". The different ways in which the various skills can be taught are limited only by the ingenuity and imagination of the instructor. Therefore, the following examples relating to the use of basic equipment should be used as guidance and not as 'Tablets of Stone'.

The mask

Students should be briefed on the function of the diving mask. However, it is only necessary to explain that the eye is designed to work in air and not in water, consequently the 'wearing of an air space' in front of the eyes will enable the student to see clearly underwater (the physics will be explained in a lecture). Before fitting the mask you should explain that hair under the seal will allow water to enter, and that if the mask strap is adjusted too tightly this will cause discomfort and distort the seal.

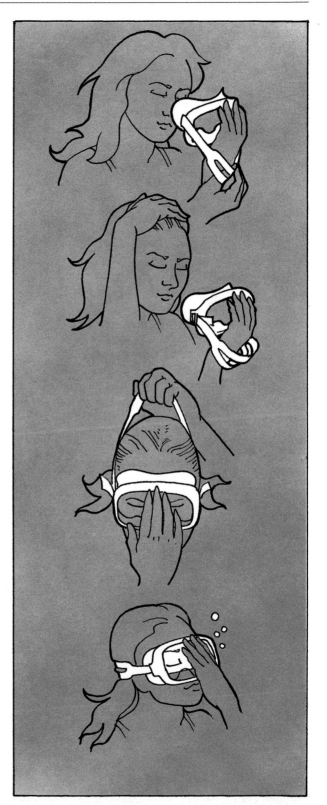

Figure 82 Mask fitting sequence – four steps.

Also that a proprietary demisting agent or saliva should be applied to the face plate and rinsed prior to use to reduce mask fogging.

Demonstrate the act of fitting the mask slowly so that they can identify each component part, this enables you to correct your students' performance before a mistake is made. Once the mask is fitted correctly, allow the students to submerge their heads briefly. Should any water enter their masks, teach them to simply ease the bottom seal from their face and allow the water to drain away. This should avoid the temptation to remove the mask totally every time a small amount of water enters. This technique is only valid when their heads are out of the water!

Clearing the mask underwater involves a more advanced technique, although, it is simply a matter of displacing water with exhaled air through the nose into the mask. It is worth noting that a similar method is required to avoid mask squeeze.

The snorkel

Demonstrate the correct fitting of the snorkel by placing it either under the mask strap or attaching it by means of a snorkel keeper. Pay particular attention to the fact that the snorkel should be nearly perpendicular to the surface of the water when being worn, looking downwards and forwards from the front swimming position. Ensure that they are not gripping the mouthpiece lugs too tightly, and that the mouthpiece seal is positioned in front of the teeth and behind the lips.

Initially, let the students breathe through the snorkel without putting their heads in the water, emphasizing the need to concentrate on exhalation, as well as inhalation. When you are satisfied that they are comfortable and breathing easily, instruct them to grasp the top of the snorkel and submerge until they feel the water touch their hand, then to inhale and exhale a predetermined number of times, and then surface. In this way you reduce the risk of water entering the snorkel, and control the time they spend submerged.

Snorkel clearing may be introduced in a similar way, by giving the students a new experience in a controlled fashion. Your approach could be to explain the principle of air displacing water, and then to demonstrate the effect of exhaling forcefully into a flooded snorkel; students could mimic this skill without needing to submerge by flooding the snorkel while holding the mouthpiece closed, and then quickly fitting and clearing. As confidence grows, clearing can be attempted with the snorkel fitted in its normal position. Displacement clearing can be initiated as the lesson progresses and their confidence grows.

The fins

Fins should be described as an extension of the pointed foot presenting a large surface area to the water, their purpose is not solely to make you swim faster, but to provide more power to move a fully equipped diver through the water.

Figure 83 Regulator sharing in shallow open water.

Figure 84 Practicing a surface dive.

Holding the side of the pool or rail, demonstrate the correct leg action keeping your legs straight with minimal bending at the knees. Have your students practice in a similar fashion while you check for faults like 'bicycling'. Remind them that fins need to be kept underwater for maximum efficiency. You will find that some people are more buoyant than others which tends to make their fins break the surface. Adding a weight belt or keeping their hands clasped behind their back will normally keep them in the correct attitude while finning.

Surface Dives

This exercise can be reduced to several component parts thereby allowing each one to be taught and practiced separately, gradually combining them all to give the end result. This method usually produces a quicker and consistently better result than simply showing the whole skill and hoping the students can copy the actions immediately. See fig 86 on page 80.

For example, a surface dive would commence by lying on the surface face down and bending the body to 90° from the waist, pointing both out-stretched arms towards the bottom of the pool. The next step is to lift both legs vertically to add weight and impetus to the descent. The final part will be to use a breaststroke pull with the arms. These four movements are gradually combined at a faster rate to produce a fluid and competent surface dive.

Personal performance

A major factor influencing the progress of the student is the quality of your personal performance in being able to demonstrate skills. You need to be more than just a good performer of a skill and it is essential that you should not only be able to execute the skill, but that you should also understand how it is done. You must analyse and evaluate the purpose of each action that constitutes the skill.

Figure 85 Improving finning technique.

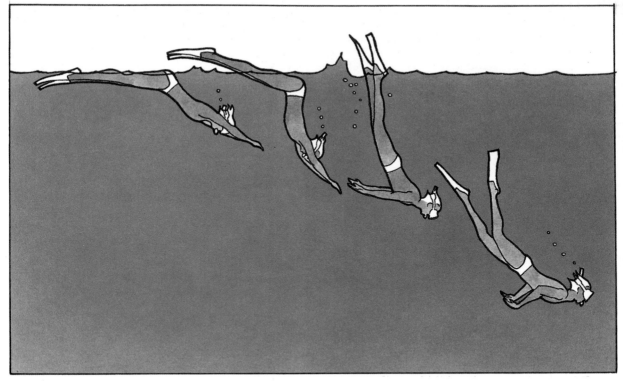

Figure 86 Surface dive broken down into its component parts.

Most experienced divers perform simple skills automatically without conscious thought. However, the instructor should guard against this familiarity with the skill.

Many apparently simple actions performed without conscious thought may be essential to the skill, and unless these are recognised by the instructor and passed on to the student they will not achieve the rapid success which they might otherwise do. For example, an attempt to carry out familiar actions with the hand not normally used by them demonstrates how complex an apparently simple action can be.

Demonstrations

The ability to imagine or sense physical actions and body movements required to achieve particular skills is an important element in skill learning. This is what your students are doing while they watch your demonstration. Learning can be further supported if students attempt to explain in their words how the skill is performed or if they watch films of the process. So, students can learn by watching others perform even before they embark on that particular part of training. Learning in this way is known as kinaesthetic imagery, that is the ability to imagine or sense in the muscles, the movement and responses that make up the skill.

Depending on the skill being taught, it is sometimes useful to demonstrate the skill at two different paces. Firstly, the actual pace which gives a clear picture of the ultimate objective and sets the standard for the students' performance, and secondly, a demonstration at a teaching pace which the student can clearly see the significance of all the movements and steps which make up the skill. In this demonstration, movements should be slowed down, repeated and exaggerated in order to emphasize their different features.

For the demonstration to be effective it is essential that all students in the teaching group are positioned so that they can clearly see your demonstration and all the movements associated with it. It is easy for essential movements to be masked by your body and you may, where necessary, repeat the demonstration showing both front and side views of the skill. For surface lessons in standing depth, a commentary can accompany the demonstration so that specific points can be emphasized.

Underwater demonstrations are carried out where it is not possible for them to be accompanied by an explanation to add emphasis. Therefore, a clear and concise briefing should take place before the demonstration, which helps to overcome the lack of a running commentary, but above all, it underlines the need for a clear, positive and faultless demonstration.

During demonstrations, you should avoid the temptation to show off your own ability. Students should be left with the impression that what they are being asked to do is an easy and an achievable objective, not something that requires years of experience.

Students practice

Once interest in the skill has been established by good preparation and a clear and efficient demonstration, a state of learning readiness will have been reached by the student. They will be motivated to attempt the skill themselves.

A period of practice must follow as soon as possible after the demonstration of a skill, and during this practice you should observe the student to analyse faults and plan corrective action if required.

The duration of practice periods must also be considered carefully. If they are too short, the various parts or steps which make up the skill are only slowly brought together. If the periods are too long, the student may become bored and cold and this will reduce motivation. Skills need time to be assimilated and intervals are desirable between practice periods to avoid staleness and fatigue.

A change of activity is often enough to serve as a break between long periods of practice and particularly difficult exercises. If a class is having problems with a particular skill, give them a break from it by returning to a skill with which they were successful and develop it further; this should avoid them becoming too discouraged about their lack of progress with the new skill. A break of this sort followed by a return to the problem is often enough for them to achieve success and move forward.

Although repetition of a skill is an important part of learning, repeating an exercise over and over again to someone who is clearly having trouble mastering the skill can seriously damage their confidence and could stop further progress.

Figure 87 Surface lesson demonstrating good class control and positioning.

Figure 88 The Instructor demonstrates mask clearing to the class.

Training areas

Swimming pools

Swimming pools have a number of advantages when compared to open water, but there are a number of disadvantages.

● Swimming pools are not necessarily designed for teaching scuba.

● Space is often at a premium.

● There may be a conflict with other users.

● The acoustics of an indoor pool may make communication difficult.

Open water

On the other hand, teaching in open water also has its disadvantages:

● Weather or surface conditions may be unsuitable.

● Visibility may be variable.

● Water temperature may require protective clothing.

● The appropriate depth may be difficult to locate or access.

Whether in a pool or open water, any practical skill taught for the first time should follow this basic principle:

DRY – SURFACE – SHALLOW – DEEPER

For the purposes of practical instruction, dry means a briefing not a lecture!

Although some verbal instruction is acceptable when teaching surface skills such as lifesaving or snorkelling skills, it should not be employed during shallow or deeper exercises. These exercises are to be conducted by seeing and doing – which we established earlier as being the most effective factors in the learning process. Constant surfacing for further briefing is a sign of poor underwater communication skills, or poor demonstration skills and is not an indication of effective instruction

Before we consider the actual poolwork, let us consider the planning process which should take place prior to entering the water. Remember that everything we do as instructors can be used as a teaching opportunity for the students. Before the lesson we should consider the following:

● Choose a briefing location away from distractions.

● Points of entry and exit to and from the water and methods of entry and exit.

● Depth and area in which the exercise is to take place. (surface/underwater)

● Equipment required.

● Time available.

We must also consider:

● The students present skill level.

● The exercise.

● The progression of the lesson.

Underwater lessons

The only effective way of teaching practical skills is by demonstration. It follows that if as instructors we are found wanting in our ability to demonstrate the skill effectively, then our student will only emulate our performance. Our demonstrations need to be progressive and show the detail clearly, thereby teaching the student how to achieve the finished skill in easy stages. This means we need to fully understand the component parts which make up the whole exercise. For example, removing and re-fitting the mask underwater.

Pace

The pace of the lesson is important if the students are not to become bored. Once it has been established to your satisfaction that a skill has been performed correctly – move to the next level of the skill or a completely new skill. However do not set a pace too fast so that the students gain no more that a superficial ability in the new skill.

Control and positioning underwater

The class needs to be positioned so that they can see the instructor clearly. In the same way as briefings, position yourself with your back to the poolside side so that the students are not distracted by other water users.

Depending on the skill to be taught, the class will need to be positioned closer to you for skills involving detail i.e. mask clearing, and further away for exercises which require more room, such as assisted ascents or controlled buoyant lifts. Students positioned in a straight line and shoulder to shoulder are generally in a more controlled position to observe your demonstration. However, for some exercises it is useful to bring a student out of line in order to mimic your demonstration this enables the rest of the class to observe and learn by observation from the efforts of their fellow students. Due to over-breathing beginners generally lack the fine buoyancy control which comes with experience and often drift away from their original positions, therefore, it will be necessary for you to re-group them from time to time. Kneeling for any length of time can be uncomfortable and chilling, so vary the lesson to include some exercises which require movement.

Safety will also play a key role on the distance chosen, in that you should be able to reach and give appropriate physical assistance for each particular exercise. Often your demonstration position can be thought of as a stage, and is also the ideal place for your students to make their initial attempts at the skill, allowing the rest of the group to learn by observation. However, when it is appropriate for the whole class to perform an exercise together, do not slow progress down by individual performances.

The structure of an underwater lesson:

> **The Briefing**
> **Entry into the water**
> **The Exercise**
> **Exit from the water**
> **The Debriefing**

Fault correction and analysis

Following your demonstration the student will attempt to mimic your performance. During this period you evaluate their ability to perform the skill to see if they have reached the required standard. If the skill is not being performed correctly, you should stop the practice session and repeat the demonstration, concentrating on those parts of the skill which are going wrong, and on what action they should take to perform the skill correctly. If they continue to perform the skill incorrectly, then analyse your own performance to see whether your demonstration was clear and unambiguous, or if a further demonstration shown from a different angle will help the students to comprehend the particular skill. The practice session can then be repeated and you can continue to analyse their performance. It is essential that all skills are learnt correctly to begin with as incorrect actions become habitual and increasingly difficult to 'unlearn'.

A skill should, however, be 'over learnt' – that is practiced somewhat beyond the point where a satisfactory performance has been attained. Overlearning establishes the skill firmly in the memory and ensures that it will be there at the right level when it is needed even in an emergency situation.

In all learning situations, knowledge of personal performance following directly after the practice period is essential for progress. This will help to sustain motivation and the more specific the information given, the greater its value to the student. This emphasizes the need for clear and concise de-briefing sessions following closely upon skill practice.

Figure 89 Close for detail.

Figure 90 Distance for effect.

Teaching in Open Water

Teaching in Open Water

There is no reason why initial diver training should not take place at a suitable open water site. Conditions for basic training in open water are of course very different to those in a swimming pool, entry and exit points are not as easy as those in a pool. In temperate zones the main problems associated with open water instruction are usually cold water, low visibility, water movement and the availability of sites which can be used all year round. Nevertheless, it is possible to find suitable sites, and there is evidence to suggest that open water training does help students to adapt more readily to the diving environment.

In warmer climates there are usually few problems. An open water training area in the tropics would be clearer and warmer than many swimming pools.

This section deals with problems relating to cold water instruction and the differences associated with instruction other than in a swimming pool or sheltered warm water.

It is important to remember that when your students leave the relative safety of the swimming pool and progress to open water, the basic teaching principles you employed in the pool still apply.

Do not believe that once a student enters open water the job of the instructor is over, and that through trial and error, the student will eventually become an experienced diver.

There are clearly adjustments to be made to accommodate the differences in conditions, equipment and the new experiences to which the student will be exposed. Your ability to plan for, and anticipate these differences could determine whether your student enjoys their first experience, or abandons the sport for good. This transition from pool to the 'real thing' is important and should be planned by the instructor to be an enjoyable and memorable experience for the student.

Equipment

Venturing into open water for the first time, may involve students in wearing a number of unfamiliar pieces of equipment which were probably not used during initial training. Thermal and protective clothing, such as a dry suit, wet suit, gloves or a 'Lycra' one-piece may be totally new to the student, as may ancillary items such as a diving knife, watch, depth gauge or compass.

The function and use of some items can be explained quickly and simply while others will require longer and more detailed explanation. To teach the use of a diving compass would require a theory session, a dry-run and an open water lesson, whereas to teach the use of a diving knife could take only a few minutes. A few moments of explanation or demonstration can and will improve the students' understanding and gives you an opportunity to teach them to use it properly and safely. This also applies when instructing experienced divers in new techniques or when they are using unfamiliar or new types of equipment or safety equipment (e.g. a surface marker buoy). Above all try to ensure that the student is comfortable with any additional equipment.

Figure 91 An open water lesson in the use of a Surface Marker Buoy.

Figure 92 An opportunity to teach during a pre-dive equipment check.

Open water conditions

Teaching in cold water needs careful consideration and planning. Lessons may need to be modified so that periods of inactivity or static exercises are reduced or kept to a minimum. However, demonstrations and static exercises are a necessary part of training to begin with and therefore lesson durations may have to be limited. If students are forced to remain in the water to the point that they are suffering extreme discomfort, their motivation and attention will rapidly deteriorate. There are a number of things that can be done to minimize the discomforts of cold. Adequate thermal protection from the elements before and after divers enter the water will help to prevent chilling. Students should enter the water quickly and begin training without delay. The lesson should be planned so that periods of static exercises are interspersed with mobile exercises such as finning, and these should be increased towards the end of the lesson.

In tropical conditions, the suns rays can be very strong, and without some form of protection your students could become badly sunburnt. Wearing a T-shirt will offer some protection from the sun, but it has little thermal insulation. Although, the water temperature is generally much warmer in the tropics, prolonged submersion can still chill the body. Avoid dehydration by drinking plenty of fluids.

Accidentally brushing against coral can cause cuts or abrasions as it tends to be sharp – some corals such as fire coral, can also sting if touched.

Figure 93 A lesson in mid-water.

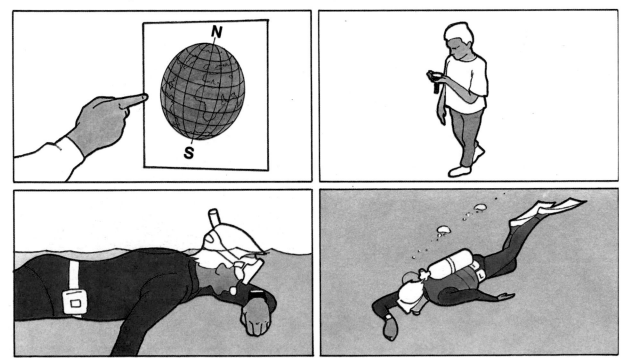

Figure 94 Progression of a lesson on navigating using a compass. – Classroom – walking a course on land – surface swimming and underwater work – more complicated later.

A skin-tight one-piece 'Lycra' suit (skin) will protect the body from the sun and provide a little warmth, and also protect you from scratches and coral burns. Poor performances towards the end of the lesson could indicate that your students are getting too cold to concentrate. Ensure that the class exits the water before anyone becomes too chilled.

Choice of site

Obviously any site chosen must be free of any strong tidal flow and, ideally, free of wave action. Usually the latter is more of a problem than the former. Students cannot be expected to cope with extreme water movement during their initial open water lessons. Remaining static while trying to perform certain skills is made more difficult with turbulent wave action.

Access to and from the water must be simple (at all states of the tide) bearing in mind that your students may be chilled and tired after their lesson. The ideal open water training area should be similar to a typical swimming pool in depth and area. A site with natural boundaries is useful in order to avoid going too far or too deep. Natural boundaries are also useful in an emergency when you may need to access the shore quickly.

Knowledge of the seabed will enable you to choose the the best spot for various training exercises. As a general rule open water lessons should begin in the same depth of water as they would in a swimming pool. In open water it is also desirable that certain exercises should start in standing depth i.e. buddy breathing, particularly if the sea conditions are difficult.

The choice of site will depend upon the type of exercise, but generally a flat seabed area with good visibility is required. If visibility deteriorates during the exercise then you should not be afraid of moving your students a short distance to a clearer site. An ideal shore based site would have a gently shelving sandy beach, this gives variable depth and, generally good visibility.

Water entry and exit

Entry to and exit from the water can present a challenging experience for those experiencing this for the first time. Always remember that it is generally easier to get in than to get out, so ensure you pick your site carefully, paying particular attention to weather and tide changes (e.g. what may be an easy entry at high water may give an extremely difficult exit at low water). A first dive should ideally be from a shore with a gently shelving bottom which allows the students to gradually increase their depth and thus keep within their capabilities, as it is not a great deal different from the depth they have experienced in the pool. If the instructional platform is a boat, ensure there are adequate arrangements to get back on board.

Remember that you, as the instructor, are ALWAYS first into the water and last out of the water to ensure you give your students adequate safety cover.

Class control

Open water, by its very definition means that you are taking students into an area of water which does not have the tightly defined boundaries encountered in the swimming pool and thus, class control is of paramount importance.

Figure 95 Wetsuits suitable for warm water.

Figure 96 Choose an area free from obstructions.

Figure 97 Leading a group of students from the front while finning backwards.

The problems usually arise when you move the group in the water to your exercise site, here your position is critical. You must at all times be in such a position that you can see ALL of your group at ALL times. Two suggested arrangements are shown in fig 97 one has the instructor in front of the group swimming backwards and the other has the instructor on the end of a line of students. The position to avoid at all cost is the one where the instructor is actually among the students, as you cannot possibly see them all at the same time.

Movement through the water should always be at the speed of the slowest in the group and the instructor should not be afraid of halting the exercise to bring the group together again. If the exercise requires a grouping on the bottom then position the group as for the pool exercise positions.

As the exercise is in open water you should ensure that you are adequately marked with a diving flag and an SMB. To avoid the SMB becoming a problem and a demonstration in entanglement it is often a good idea to attach a small weight to the SMB and deploy it to the sea traffic side of your group. It may be efficiently deployed from the surface by attaching the reel handle to the buoy and the line to the small weight, which can then be dropped from the surface at the chosen site.

Many of the skills needed by a diver will be taught in open water – whether that means from a sloping seashore, a slipway or a lake. Open water teaching also involves teaching divers skills in boats – again these can be large boats, with lots of space or small boats such as inflatable boats or rigid-hulled inflatable boats (RIBs), with restricted space.

This aspect of instructing will be dealt with under a separate heading. As with any scuba activity, lessons carried out in open water will benefit both the instructor and the student if they are planned thoroughly and well in advance of the training.

Planning

The lesson plan will need to consider a number of factors which will probably differ considerably from those which were involved during the planning of a lesson in a swimming pool. A summary of some of the most typical factors that need to be considered might include:

> Access to and from the Dive Site
> Creature Comforts
> Type of shore Entry and Exit
> Underwater Visibility
> Additional Equipment
> Class Control and Safety
> Sea State
> Other water traffic
> Other water users

Moving students to and from a swimming pool is relatively simple. Moving them to and from an open water dive site might involve a considerable amount of planning in its own right. Having arrived on-site can we arrange transport down to the waters edge? and what about parking facilities for the transport? What, if any, are the arrangements for changing? Are there toilets? Will we need to take our own refreshments or is there a convenient local source? Do we need to obtain permission from someone in order to use the dive site?

We need to consider the safest and easiest way to enter the water. The seabed is rarely flat and smooth so we will need to consider how and where to kit up particularly fitting fins. For an entry from a sloping shore, it might be better to have the students enter the water, and support each other whilst fitting their fins and then walk backwards into the deeper water. Remember that this is much safer if the students are all wearing their masks, using their snorkel or regulators and with air in their buoyancy compensators. Entry from a boat or from a jetty might easily be one of the techniques taught during swimming pool training – silent entry, step-in entry, forward roll or backward roll. Similarly, exit from the water and into the boat will have been practiced before. It is always a good idea to teach the class members an appropriate entry and exit rather than let them look after themselves and hope that it might be alright.

Underwater visibility at open water sites can vary from being 'gin-clear' to quite murky and this will need to be borne in mind when choosing a site for teaching purposes. With poor visibility, there is a limit to how much detail of the teaching of underwater skills can be undertaken. If the students cannot see the instructor properly, they will be unable to copy the demonstration. This might be partially compensated for by teaching a smaller group, so that the students and the instructor can be closer together.

Connected with the problem of underwater visibility can be the type of bottom where the exercise is going to be taught. Positioning a class on a mud bottom will certainly create a loss of visibility quite quickly. Visibility will also be impaired if the site chosen is amongst long, thick kelp.

Always ensure that the class is positioned in such a way that they are all as comfortable as possible, and can see your demonstration and that you are able to immediately carry out corrective action when needed.

Since the teaching will be taking place in open water, students should all wear full scuba equipment. It is essential that the instructor checks each and every item of equipment worn by each student to ensure that it is correctly fitted and in good working order. Also, the exercise might involve the use of other equipment, such as ropes, weights, buoys, lifting bags, etc. It is essential that any such equipment is checked thoroughly. Teaching and performing skills is much easier if the equipment is kept as simple as possible.

With some exercises, the class might be moving (i.e. use of a compass for navigation) and the instructor needs to pay particular attention to the need for control of a moving group. This can be achieved by positioning themselves just to one side of the group or just ahead of the group, with the instructor swimming on their back or slightly above the group.

Control of the class underwater is really the same problem as it was in the swimming pool, taking into account the possible problems caused by variable underwater visibility and bottom quality. Students should be aware of what to do in the unlikely event of separation underwater – "One up, All up"! Control

underwater is difficult if the student is buoyant and is therefore moving about throughout the demonstration.

During the equipment check, it is useful for the instructor to ensure that each student can control their buoyancy and is able to stay in one place easily, but is also able to achieve neutral buoyancy or controlled positive buoyancy when needed.

A group of trainees underwater can often be uncomfortable with the prospect of being on the bottom in a large expanse of open water. In these circumstances, a great degree of comfort can be generated by the use of a datum line. The most common form of the datum line is the surface marker buoy at the end of a weighted line. This gives a point of reference and also a meeting point on the surface, as well as warning surface traffic that underwater activities are taking place.

Shore based lessons and dry-runs

Shore based lessons and dry-runs fulfil two separate functions but share the common characteristic, in that they are performed in air. This allows the instructor to converse with the students throughout the lesson and hence the usual demo/mimic technique can be supplemented by coaching techniques.

Figure 98 Launching a boat requires the co-ordination of a number of skills.

Shore based lessons are generally used to teach a specific skill or activity which would, in the normal course of diving, take place on the shore. Examples of such activities are; entries and exits to and from the water in different conditions, boat launching/recovery and rescue skills such as incident management and casualty recovery from the water. Dry-runs, on the other hand, are used as a progressive step in learning the theory behind a particular skill and it's performance underwater.

Typically these are more 'applied' skills, such as navigation and searching, which involve the mastery of equipment additional to that needed just to swim and survive underwater e.g. ropes, buoys, weights etc.

Shore based lessons

Shore based lessons form an entity in themselves. They start with a briefing which will follow the normal SEEDS format, although the signals and discipline elements will be much less comprehensive than for a lesson which would be carried out underwater.

Many of the skills lend themselves to the traditional instructor demo/student mimic technique. During the student mimic, however, the instructor can give further verbal guidance to the students to ensure successful acquisition of the skill. This is particularly important where the skill is quite complex and requires the co-ordination of the efforts of a number of people e.g. boat launching.

Some skills, however, are less specific and a coaching technique is more appropriate. An example of this is rescue management skills. An instructor demonstration of dealing with a particular scenario is a valuable tool in demonstrating the concepts involved. Because of the infinite variety in the circumstances of real life incidents, the concepts, rather than the detail are the important lessons to be learnt. Having demonstrated the application of the concepts of one particular scenario the instructor can build on this by coaching the students through the application of those concepts of a series of different scenarios. The key feature of coaching in this instance is that the instructor does not tell the students what they should be doing but guides their thought processes, so that they are successfully able to make that determination themselves.

At the end of the lesson the instructor will debrief the students reiterating the lessons learnt to bring the lesson to a close.

Figure 99 Compass practice before diving.

Figure 100 Rescue assessment in open water.

Dry-runs

Dry-runs are used in circumstances where the basics of a complex skill can be learnt on dry land before taking that skill underwater. This is a means of ensuring a progressive build up of the skill in a benign environment before adding the additional burden of performing the skill underwater, cluttered up with a full set of scuba equipment. The purpose of the dry-run is to improve the efficiency of learning when underwater and should only be used when it can contribute to this process. If a skill can be more effectively taught underwater then that is where it should be taught.

In some instances the skill can be practiced in the dry. An example of this is the use of a compass, where the precise use of the compass can be practiced on land before progressing to exactly the same exercises on the surface or underwater. In other instances the dry-run will familiarize the students with a particular arrangement of equipment before it is used underwater e.g. lifting bags etc.,

As the dry-run is the starting point for the lesson it should commence with a student briefing. This should not only explain the relevance of the skill to be learnt but also the relevance of the dry-run to the process of learning and how it will relate to the subsequent 'wet' portion of the lesson.

The elements of the dry-run should then be worked through, progressively building up to a basis on which the lesson can be taken underwater. In effect, the dry-run is an extended form of the 'Exercise' part of the normal briefing. The dry-run will usually take the form of an instructor demonstration followed by student mimic.

As with the shore based lessons the instructor obviously has the advantage of being able to talk to the students about the skill and its relevance throughout this part of the lesson.

Once the dry-run is completed satisfactorily the instructor should then brief the students on the 'wet' part of the lesson. This briefing will follow a traditional 'SEEDS' brief but should reiterate the link between what has been completed in the dry-run and that which is about to be carried out underwater. Skills which warrant a dry-run are typically the more advanced skills. This means that the students will have a reasonable amount of diving experience. It is important that the instructor recognises this in the briefing and does not treat the students as diving students. It is only in respect of the particular skill that they are to be taught that the students are novices.

Where additional equipment has to be used, a significant element of the briefing will involve the logistics of how the equipment is to be transported from the shore to the actual site and back.

Underwater lessons

Underwater lessons can vary quite dramatically in their scope, from a students first dive in shallow, sheltered water to the further extension of an advanced diver's experience to greater depth or in more complex techniques. In the earlier stages of a diver's training these lessons tend to evolve around progressing personal diving techniques learnt in a swimming pool or sheltered water environment into progressively less benign conditions. As experience builds, the

Figure 101 A lesson at greater depth – simulated decompression stop.

lessons evolve to introduce more advanced techniques which may involve either pure diving, or personal, skills such as diving to progressively greater depths, or applied skills, such as searches or lifting objects.

Whatever the lesson, it is important that the activity is properly planned as a teaching exercise which will ensure a successful outcome for the student. Too often teaching is regarded as an activity which only takes place in the pool or sheltered water, with the idea that students are only assessed in open water. Students are therefore left to carry out an exercise and are subsequently told what they have done wrong. Apart from being a negative approach, which will provide little value or enjoyment to the student, it can also be dangerous, depending upon the particular exercise.

Teaching techniques

Teaching techniques for underwater lessons vary with the scope of the lessons concerned. For a students' initial underwater lessons the demonstration/mimic technique will most frequently be used and works well where specific personal techniques are concerned. This is really an extension of the teaching that the student has already undergone in the more sheltered water environment, and the skills concerned readily lend themselves to this technique.

As the lessons progress to more advanced personal or applied skills this technique may not be possible, or may be inappropriate for other reasons. For instance, when students are being introduced to decompression diving, it is impossible to carry out a demonstration of a decompression stop without the student actually doing one at the same time. In this situation the student must therefore be coached through the procedure. Safety can still be maintained by making the stop a simulated one rather than a real decompression stop. When you take students to a depth beyond their previous experience it is impossible to demonstrate and consequently a coaching technique is more appropriate.

Where techniques have already been experienced several times during a progression the initial demonstration/mimic technique may not remain the optimum technique. Where, for instance, a search technique has already been the subject of a dry-run and shallow water lessons, a further demonstration in deeper water may not be necessary. Although the students will have done the exercise before, they will still not be entirely familiar with it and consequently a coaching technique, where the instructor guides the students through the exercise to ensure that they complete it successfully, will be more appropriate.

Class control

Effective class control is an essential element of instruction. With the progression in the complexity of the lessons being taught, the greater mobility involved in many of the exercises and the widening scope of conditions under which the teaching will be carried out there is considerable scope for disruption of the lesson if effective class control is not maintained. This subject merits adequate forethought and preparation prior to the lesson.

Figure 102 Octopus sharing exercise.

Figure 103 Drawing the students' attention to marine life.

Lesson structure

The basic lesson structure used in pool or sheltered water lessons is still appropriate to more advanced lessons, although the considerations that need to be taken into account for each element expand somewhat.

Briefing

This will contain all the elements covered by 'SEEDS' although, because of diving conditions or the more complex nature of the exercises will generally be more complex. In particular, where the lesson aims to introduce students to a technique where unfamiliar equipment is to be used – such as compass navigation or searches – the Exercise portion of the briefing may need to expand to become a dry-run. This dry-run element could, be a substantial portion of the overall lesson as it is essential to the smooth progress of the subsequent underwater part of the lesson. It is important to ensure that the briefing addresses those elements relevant to the lesson and to the students' level of knowledge. On their early lessons, students will need reminding about ear clearing whereas a group of experienced divers would not, but would need a detailed briefing on equipment they have not seen before.

Kitting up

This will include the normal personal equipment and buddy' checks but will also need to encompass any additional 'task' equipment required for the lesson. It would be embarrassing to discover, once underwater, that the lifting bag vital to the lesson had been left behind, so the logistics of how the equipment is to be conveyed to the dive site and by who should be clearly understood.

Water entry

The type of access to the water will need to be taken into account, as will the precise location of where the lesson is to be carried out in order to ensure that the appropriate conditions are obtained. As the transit from the point of entry to the lesson location will be longer, either due to distance or depth, good class control will be necessary to ensure that the class remain together. In particular, while on the surface other water users will also need to be considered. The amount of time taken for this element of the lesson should not be underestimated and should have been taken into account in the lesson plan.

Demonstration

Water conditions may be considerably different to those for earlier lessons, especially where the earlier lessons have been carried out in a swimming pool. Visibility may be reduced due to plankton, suspended matter or just due to the lower light levels at depth. Any bottom sediment stirred up by the class will further reduce visibility. The class will therefore need to be kept in a much tighter group both for the instructor to maintain control, and for the students to be able to see the demonstration.

Mimic

Many of the same considerations apply as for the demonstration with the added requirement that the instructor can not only see the students' performance but is also in the best position to intervene when safety demands. This is especially true in lessons involving ascents, where it is essential that uncontrolled ascents are anticipated and prevented.

Correction

Considerations for this are the same as for the demonstration and mimic. Depending on the teaching technique employed, especially where a dry-run has been incorporated into the lesson or where a specific demonstration is not possible, the demonstration, mimic and correction may become combined as the instructor coaches the students through the exercise.

Exit

The ascent and transit to the point of exit will require further tight class control. Not only is it essential to ensure that all the class surface close to any Surface Marker Buoy used, but also to ensure that the class remains together until they have left the water. The exit procedure will also require that any additional equipment used as part of the lesson will need to be retrieved.

Debrief

Generally this will be more effective if done immediately while the exercise is fresh in the students' minds. If, however, this means standing around in extreme climatic conditions, either hot or cold, it will generally be better to delay the debrief a short time until the class can reassemble in a suitably sheltered environment. In these circumstances a delayed debrief in comfort will be far more effective.

The above structure provides a framework which can be applied to any lesson. Each of the elements is always present in one form or another, although the detail of each element may vary considerably from one lesson to another.

Teaching divers to enjoy themselves

One aspect of teaching that is often overlooked is that of merely teaching less experienced divers to observe what is happening around them underwater. All the techniques learned in scuba training are merely a means to an end – to enjoy the underwater world. This aspect warrants just as much attention by scuba instructors as teaching the diving skills required. Many divers miss seeing a lot of interesting objects underwater such as parts of wrecked ships or marine life purely because they have not been taught how to look for them. Many divers also inadvertently cause a lot of destruction underwater because they have not been taught how to avoid causing damage with their fins or when grabbing hold of rocks covered in encrusting life. The protection of the underwater environment so that we will be able to continue to enjoy it in the future is an important aspect of diver training that is most effectively carried out underwater. Although not a formal 'skill' as such, it is still an aspect which can be approached using the same lesson structure although on a much more informal basis.

Figure 104 Practicing compass navigation.

Figure 105 Instructor awaiting the arrival of the group.

Figure 105a Keep the group together on the surface.

Equipment

In the initial stages of open water training the equipment used will be the personal equipment needed just to survive underwater. As training progresses and the divers experience increases, ancillary equipment needed to carry out specific tasks underwater or even equipment needed to accurately locate the dive site and to transport divers to it, will be introduced. While most students will quickly acquire their own personal diving equipment the equipment resources needed for the more advanced lessons will need to be organised by the instructor. In some instances this will be because, until they have undergone the training, the trainees will not know anything about the equipment required or particularly with the more expensive equipment, it is normally club owned or chartered.

Personal diving equipment

Teaching in the use of personal diving equipment commences long before entry into the water. The example set by the instructors own equipment and the way in which it is handled it will influence students in their attitude towards their own equipment. It is essential, therefore, that your equipment is in good condition and that you treat it with the respect that it deserves.

Immediately prior to water entry the buddy check is carried out. This is an essential element of all diving lessons. Not only does it ensure that students learn that this is an essential part of all diving but it also reinforces the importance of this check for more experienced and more capable students.

By their nature in-water lessons concerning personal diving equipment will require that the students are equipped with their normal diving equipment. With the different standards of equipment available it is important that you determine beforehand that your equipment and that of your students is compatible and appropriate to the lesson concerned.

Ancillary equipment

The scope of this ancillary equipment is very broad ranging from equipment as simple as a wrist compass, through oxygen administration equipment and lifting equipment to fully equipped boats.

Even for initial lessons for which the students only require their own personal diving equipment there are additional considerations from the instructors viewpoint. In addition to your own personal equipment you will find a surface marker buoy a useful and important item. This will fulfil two functions. The first is the normal safety function of providing a warning to other water users of the divers presence. Even for very early lessons which may only be taking place in chest deep water, the proximity of the class heads to the surface makes this an indispensable item when other water users are around. The second function is that of providing a position datum for the class underwater. To avoid the surface marker buoy becoming an encumbrance, rather than having the reel attached to your equipment in the normal way, it is preferable to have it attached to

a small weight which can be placed on the bottom close to you. You can then move around the class easily and the line can be used as a datum in exercises such as assisted ascents without the need for you to continually reel the line in and out.

For lessons introducing the students to ancillary equipment the scope and nature of this equipment needs to be considered in the light of the objective of the particular lesson. While the ultimate objective of the training may be, for example, to lift a very heavy object using a large lifting bag the technique itself can be learned in the early stages with much more lightweight and compact equipment. Once the technique itself has been mastered in shallow, sheltered conditions the training can progress to less benign conditions and can introduce heavier objects and larger lifting bags. An appropriate standard of equipment therefore needs to be determined which will satisfy the training objective of each particular stage in the training. Particularly for initial stages carried out from the shore the logistical implications also benefit from a simplified equipment configuration.

While obtaining much of the necessary equipment for many more advanced lessons is an organizational or logistical exercise there are many common items of equipment which can be utilized, particularly for many of the earlier stages in the lesson progressions. The following are examples of such equipment with typical uses:

- *A selection of weights of varying sizes and shapes*
  Lighter weights (4 – 6 kg.) for anchoring Surface Marker Buoys, medium sized weights (6 – 10 kg.) for constructing light shotlines for shore based search lessons or to be lifted in initial lifting exercises, heavy weights (10 – 20 kg.) for constructing shot lines for use in deeper water or where water movement is a factor.

- *A selection of buoys of various sizes*
  Smaller buoys for use as Surface Marker Buoys, for light weight shotlines for shore based exercises or with a small weight attached for use in boat handling exercises practicing diver pick-up. Larger buoys for constructing heavier shotlines for more advanced searches etc.

- *Reels*
  For use with Surface Marker Buoys, as distance or datum lines for search exercises, for teaching the use of delayed SMBs etc.

- *A selection of ropes and lines of varying strengths*
  To make up buddy lines, shot lines, decompression lines, search lines etc.

- *A selection of snap-shackles of various sizes*
  Pre-attached to simplify the connection of ropes and equipment by eliminating the need to tie knots underwater.

● *Compass boards*
    Underwater slates or notepads - enable the instructor to take his lesson plan underwater and to record notes underwater for the subsequent debrief.

This list is by no means an exhaustive one. In many cases more than one item of equipment will be needed for a lesson for example where Surface Marker Buoys are required to mark both the start and end of a compass navigation exercise. Some items may also perform multiple functions such as one reel being required as part of a light weight shot line for a search exercise while a second reel is required as the distance line on which the divers will swim.

The scuba instructor will have acquired many such items of ancillary equipment for normal diving activities but increasing the scope and amount of the equipment available will facilitate more effective instruction.

Equipment transport
For lessons involving the use of such additional equipment logistic considerations become significant. While the equipment itself will often be introduced to the students during a dry run it will still need to be transported to the location of the exercise.

For shore diving exercises this will most likely entail swimming it out. By careful planning beforehand this can be incorporated into the lesson by distributing the responsibility for transporting the various pieces of equipment around the students. This not only spreads the effort but gives the students a greater feeling of involvement. It must also be remembered that what is taken out will also need to be brought back!

For boat based lessons the equipment will need to be stowed in an appropriate location. This will need to be done so that the equipment needed first is most readily available. How the equipment is to be used once at the diving site also needs pre-planning. Shotlines for instance are likely to be positioned from the boat and hence will need to be used before the divers kit up with their personal diving equipment. Other equipment will need to be carried by the divers and hence will need to be accessible after the divers are fully kitted or may need to be handed to them once they are in the water. As with shore based

lessons the logistics of who will carry which item of equipment needs to be pre-arranged. The recovery and stowing of the equipment at the end of the lesson requires the same planning and organisation.

The planning of the logistical aspects of these lessons is in itself a teaching opportunity and should be incorporated as part of the lesson.

Where additional equipment is required underwater it is inevitable that additional time will be required to prepare the equipment, transport it to the location of the exercise and to subsequently recover it. This needs to be taken into account at the planning stage and an appropriate time allowance included.

Figure 105b Preparing a Shotline for the exercise.

Depths and ratios

The depths at which the various diving skills are taught generally follow a progression, with skills initially being taught in safe shallow water. Once the basics of the skill have been mastered this capability is then built upon by generally progressing to less benign conditions and deeper water. Depth is therefore one aspect of training progression, but one which can have safety implications.

As has already been seen, practical training can take place on dry land in the form of the dry-run. In-water lessons then follow and it is the depths appropriate to these lessons that we must now consider.

Surface lessons

Some lessons, by their very nature, have to take place at the surface. Boat handling and the administration of Artificial Ventilation while towing a casualty are good examples of this type of lesson.

The surface can, however, be one step along the way to taking a skill underwater. How to clear water from a snorkel can easily be taught by flooding the snorkel at the surface in advance of the student progressing to surface dives. A further example of such a lesson is compass navigation. Having learnt the basics of how to use a compass on the solid base of land, students can progress to carrying out exactly the same exercises, but in the less stable environment provided by the water. At this point it will be of benefit to the student to be able to look up occasionally to monitor their progress towards their target. Any errors due to the way the student is holding or setting the compass can thus be corrected where the instructor has the facility to use verbal instructions. The in-water technique can thus be mastered before introducing the additional demands of repeating the skill underwater.

Shallow water

The term shallow water is a relative term and can be interpreted in this context as the minimum practical depth in which the skill being taught can be performed. The actual depth will therefore vary from skill to skill.

Some basic techniques only require that the student is fully submerged. The first time that a student is taught mask and mouthpiece clearing requires water as shallow as chest depth. By kneeling down the student is fully submerged but with ready access to the surface for both confidence and safety considerations.

Other more mobile skills also only require a similar depth of water. Taking again the example of compass navigation, once the student is submerged, even in as little as 1.5m of water, they will no more be able to see their target until they are very close to it than if they were in much deeper water. The immediate objective has thus been achieved.

Safety considerations require that some initial skills training occurs in slightly deeper water. Surface dives, for instance, need a depth of 2m or so. In shallower water there will not only be insufficient depth for the skill to be performed without colliding with the bottom, making it counterproductive from an instructional viewpoint, but this will also introduce the potential for injury.

For some lessons the depth may be dictated by the physical size of some of the equipment used. Lessons involving lifting objects, for instance, will require a minimum depth which is adequate to inflate the lifting bag sufficiently to cause the object being lifted to clear the bottom.

In the swimming pool, the location of the lesson can usually be tailored to provide the appropriate depth of water but elsewhere it is inevitable that for some lessons a compromise will have to be achieved. While it may be possible to teach a basic skill in a certain minimum depth, this depth may not be available for a number of reasons. The physical geography of the site may not provide exactly this depth, or wave action may be resulting in far too much water movement or bottom sediment being disturbed resulting in poor visibility. The decision that must be made in these circumstances is whether going slightly deeper will adversely affect safety. If safety is not an issue, then the additional depth of water needs only to be taken account of in the structure of the lesson. If, however, it is likely that safety will be unacceptably prejudiced, then the compromise will be to change the lesson to one which is appropriate to both the student and the conditions available.

Deeper water

While the basics skills can be mastered in very shallow water they will inevitably require progression to deeper water. For pure diving skills this progression may occur over a period of time as part of the students gradual build up of experience.

Simple skills such as mask and regulator clearing can only be repeated in deeper water once the students' overall experience has increased to allow this. Applied skills, such as navigation etc. being learnt by more experienced divers can be progressed into deeper water much more rapidly.

The progression to deeper water introduces the student to new aspects of the skills concerned. For basic skills there is the need for confidence building, combined with the need to repeat certain skills periodically to ensure that the student remains in practice.

Other skills are altered subtly by increasing depth, changes which it is important for the student to understand. For instance, as depth increases, the rate at which buoyancy devices inflate is reduced requiring more positive introduction of air to adjust buoyancy. The greater amount of air introduced then requires more positive venting as it expands during the later ascent.

By its very nature shallow water is a much more benign environment than deeper water, but not because of the depth alone. The most benign environment is that of the swimming pool with its clear, warm water, its flat progressively shelving bottom and its limited area. As depth increases the locations become of necessity much less sheltered and consequently introduce much more variable water and geographic conditions. These conditions will need to be taken into account when planning lessons such that the student is properly taught not only to adapt to the increased depth, but also to cope with the wider range of conditions experienced.

Increased depth effects of nitrogen narcosis. Student divers should be adequately briefed and then exposed to deep water under controlled conditions involving moderate increments beyond depths which they have recently dived. These dives should be undertaken in the company of an experienced instructor accustomed to diving to the required depth.

Decompression considerations

Decompression considerations are generally regarded as a factor met only in deeper diving, although in the instructional environment this is not necessarily the case. Teaching some skills such as, assisted ascents or controlled buoyant lifts can involve decompression considerations in very shallow water due to multiple ascent or ascent rate considerations.

Ascent rates

Ascent rates become more critical the nearer the diver approaches the surface, the last 6m of the ascent requiring one minute. Such a slow ascent rate is unrealistic for rescue ascents, and in a real emergency would be of a lesser consideration. The effect of ascent rate on decompression requirements cannot, however, be ignored in the training environment. For initial training taking place in less than 6m of water, such training should be planned before any other diving to greater depth. Ascending at a faster rate is acceptable provided that no one involved has dived deeper than 6m in the previous 16 hours – i.e. there is no residual nitrogen consideration.

As such exercises progress deeper, then the ascents should be terminated at a depth of 6m. A normal ascent to the surface can then be completed, or a descent can be made for further repeats.

Repeat ascents

Repeated ascents and descents should be avoided wherever possible. Training should be planned such that the number of repeats is minimized and wherever possible spread over a number of occasions, rather than completed in one intensive session. Where circumstances prevent this, any repeat ascents/descents should be completed as early in the dive as possible. Each ascent, irrespective of whether it is commenced from a depth greater than or less than 6m, should be considered as a completed dive. Any subsequent descent, whether this be commenced from the surface or from a previous ascent terminated at 6m, should be treated as a subsequent dive and decompression requirements adjusted accordingly.

Ratios

There is no set ratio of students to instructors appropriate to any one lesson. The variation in conditions that may be experienced dictates that each circumstance is evaluated on its own merits. The factors which have to be taken into account are; the subject of the lesson itself, the experience of the students, and the conditions under which the lesson will be conducted. All these must be considered against training effectiveness and safety with the latter having the overriding consideration.

Figure 106 Identifying transits from a large boat.

Figure 107 Learning how to use navigational equipment .

In general, higher student:instructor ratios are acceptable in shallow water. Practical class considerations imposed by the blinkering effect of vision through a facemask dictate that, even under ideal conditions, classes should generally be limited to a student :instructor ratio of 4:1 with a greater ratio only under exceptional circumstances. As depth increases, conditions become less benign, or for students of little experience this ratio will need to reduce if training effectiveness and safety are not to be prejudiced. For some lessons safety considerations will dictate a reduction in the ratio to 1:1. Such circumstances could include a students first deep dive or even a simple skill taught under conditions of poor visibility.

Teaching from boats

Teaching from boats offers both its challenges and its opportunities. While the scope for teaching opportunities widens, the environmental conditions under which that teaching will be carried out also diversify. More thought has therefore to be given both to capitalising on the opportunities offered and to mitigating the effect on the lesson of the distractions of the environment.

Teaching from boats involves a broad range of teaching topics and, as a consequence, a broad range of teaching techniques. The topics involved can be grouped into three loose categories depending upon the nature of the topic, pre-planned lessons, planned and unplanned teaching opportunities.

Pre-planned lessons

These lessons involve the teaching of a specific skill, such as boat handling, and form a discrete objective in their own right. The lessons are thoroughly planned beforehand and may have been preceded by a certain amount of related theory or dry practical instruction. These lessons are generally in the form of instructor demonstration followed by student practice. A running commentary can be kept up by the instructor throughout the demonstration to amplify various points. When appropriate, during student practice, the instructor can verbally coach the student through particular elements.

This is particularly useful where the student needs to learn to anticipate certain events, such as reducing power when cresting a wave. In a small open boat careful thought must be given to the position of the instructor relative to the student, to ensure that any verbal instructions given will be heard above the noise of the wind, waves or engine. In larger boats selection of an appropriate location on the boat away from engine noise and sheltered from the elements is generally possible. For boat handling exercises in particular, the instructor must also be positioned such that, during student practice, the instructor can intervene quickly and effectively when safety demands.

Planned opportunities

During the course of normal scuba diving many opportunities to teach present themselves and can be taken advantage of. Some of these opportunities can be anticipated and consequently planned for in advance.

For example, an inexperienced diver in their first boat dive will clearly need instruction on a number of aspects. These start with where to stow equipment, and progress through kitting up in the confines of a boat,

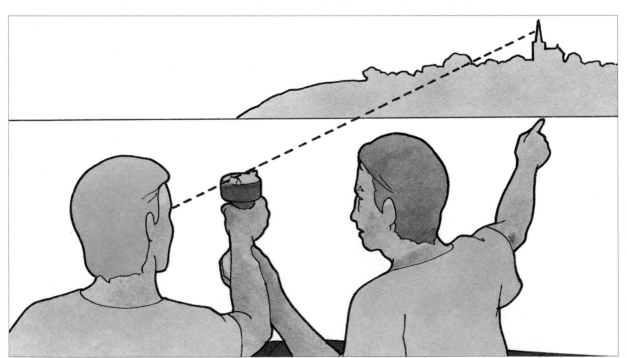

Figure 108 Lining up on a transit from a RIB.

water entry methods, descent procedures, ascent procedures and re-entering the boat. All of these aspects will be different to the diver's previous experience of shore diving and are entirely predictable. These can, therefore, be planned in advance to give a thoroughly enjoyable introduction to boat diving. As all these elements are unavoidable parts of the dive, failure to plan ahead can only have a detrimental effect on the conduct of the dive and hence the enjoyment of all concerned.

Prior thought can also identify other activities which will need to be carried out as part of the overall scuba diving activity which will provide opportunities for instruction – even of some of the more experienced divers. For instance, if a shot line is to be used to mark a particular site, it is useful to get divers who have never had to make up and lay a shot involved in those activities. They will then learn the relevant techniques and will in future not rely on other divers with the appropriate skills being available to shot a site for them.

Unplanned opportunities

Many opportunities present themselves with little or no warning but nevertheless, if used correctly, allow some form of instruction to be given. The extent of this instruction and how it is achieved will vary dramatically from opportunity to opportunity.

Any activity which increases the knowledge or skills of the divers involved, and hence helps them to get more enjoyment out of their scuba diving, is a form of instruction.

This may involve nothing more than the identification of a particular buoy that the boat is passing with a brief explanation of what the buoy indicates. This may well occur as part of the normal flow of conversation with the recipients of the information not even realising that they have in fact been taught anything – a sort of surreptitious teaching!

Other topics may be more complex but can generally be accommodated within the normal diving activities, provided that you confine yourself to skills or information that are directly relevant at the time. These activities will gain the attention of the divers concerned. Attempts to expand beyond this, or to go deeply into the theory, will quickly result in a loss of interest as the divers' attention returns to the diving in hand.

Teaching techniques

The range of teaching techniques which can be used to teach in boats is as varied as the opportunities that occur. Where specific lessons are planned or opportunities are entirely predictable then the appropriate lesson structure can be thought through beforehand.

Exactly how the lesson will be conducted or the opportunity handled can be decided in advance and the appropriate teaching technique selected. These circumstances often involve the traditional demo/mimic approach.

Unplanned opportunities, by definition, involve little or no time for preparation. If the opportunity is not to be lost the instructor must have in mind a number of strategies which can be applied to the situation. These strategies cannot be too detailed if they are to cope with the wide variety of circumstances which may be encountered. The common factor, however, is the mental attitude necessary to look out for such opportunities rather than just to continue diving and let them pass by. The opportunities need to be identified relative to the present experience or knowledge of the divers concerned. Clearly anything that they know or are familiar with is not a teaching opportunity but anything which is in any way new most certainly is. Typical strategies which can be applied include, but are not limited to, the following:

● Explain what there is to be seen and what it means point out to divers anything that may be beyond their present experience or knowledge.

The area of rougher water ahead indicating shallower water which is to be avoided.

The approaching solid line of clouds indicating a weather front, and hence an imminent weather change.

The line of pot markers which is to be avoided to prevent fouling the boat's propeller (and in consideration of diver/fisherman relations!).

Identifying the birds colonising the cliff faces around the dive site.

These and many more instances will all contribute to increasing the divers knowledge and enjoyment of scuba diving and the diving environment.

● Explain what you are doing and why you are doing it – instead of just carrying out some task or action explain to the others present what you are doing and the reasons for it.

For instance, explaining how you are using two transits to position the boat over the diving site would show how lining up two marks provides a transit, why you have chosen one particular transit to run in on relative to the wind and sea, how to adjust the boats speed as the transit intersection point is approached and how to identify precisely when the boat is above the dive site. If the other divers present are used to using transits the explanation would be tailored to showing them the precise marks to be used so that they will be able to find the site for themselves in future.

Involve other divers in doing things – with a little encouragement and direction divers can be involved in a controlled way in activities which are beyond their previous experience. Activities such as helping to launch and then load the boat, helping to prepare a shot line and helping with the dive marshalling are all good examples. In each case the particular tasks will need to be kept small and simple initially and the divers will need specific instructions about what they are to do. They will also need to be monitored to ensure that they carry out the tasks correctly but by participating they will have learnt new skills which can be called upon in future.

These are only a few examples of the opportunities and teaching techniques possible. In many instances the instruction can appear to be just a natural part of the conversation or activity of going diving. This surreptitious form of teaching also allows the divers concerned to lose the feeling of always being the student and to feel more of an equal in the group. They will accumulate knowledge and skills without feeling that they are under instruction, but will notice a real benefit in their increased enjoyment of the sport.

Figure 109 Student gaining experience using a Surface Marker Buoy and reel.

Progressive instruction

The whole object of instruction is to increase the students' level of knowledge or skill. If too much is presented at any one time they will find it difficult to comprehend or to assimilate the skill due to information overload. The way to avoid this, and which ensures the training is carried out most efficiently, is known as progressive instruction.

What constitutes progressive instruction?

Progressive instruction starts by establishing a point to which the student can relate. Every student will have some existing knowledge or skill with which they are familiar and which can be used as a basis on which to build towards the new knowledge or skill.

The new information or skill is then broken down into small manageable steps, the first of which builds directly on the starting level and each subsequent step building directly on its preceding step. Only when each step is fully assimilated does the lesson progress to the next. By working through the steps in this way the new knowledge or skill is built up progressively.

Complex topics or skills can be broken down into their component elements. The greater the complexity the greater the number of steps in the progression.

Progression in practice

The potential for the application of progression to a lesson can be illustrated by considering both an example of teaching a very basic skill and an example of teaching a very complex skill.

A simple skill

The ability to be able to clear water from the facemask is a very basic skill which must be mastered early in the student diver's training. It is, however, a fairly stressful exercise for someone for whom being underwater and breathing through a mouthpiece is still a fairly new experience. If the student is to be taught the new skill of mask clearing successfully it is necessary to consider all the different aspects which will be of concern to the student and to address each aspect one at a time.

● The need to breathe underwater without a facemask this can be practiced first of all with the student in very shallow water holding on to a secure handhold. Without a facemask the student commences breathing from the regulator and, once a regular rhythm is established, slowly squats down in the water until the water level covers their mouth and nose. Should any difficulty ensue the student merely has to raise their head a short distance to be able to breathe normally through the nose. As confidence is gained the student submerges the whole of their face underwater and breathes through the regulator for a longer period of time.

The need to surface if the exercise goes wrong is both a psychological consideration for the student and a safety consideration for the instructor. If the exercise is carried out in water which is just deep enough to cover the student's head when knelt down the student will have the confidence of knowing that all that is necessary to regain the surface is to stand up. The instructor will have the confidence of knowing that in such a short ascent the risk of lung damage, should the student hold their breath, is minimal.

● Removing a mask underwater is a big step for someone who has not done it before – neither is it necessary just to teach the technique of mask-clearing. This is best done by first introducing just a little water to partially flood the mask. Once the technique of clearing this water has been mastered, the exercise can be extended by more extensive flooding of the mask until it is fully flooded. The final step will be fully remove the facemask to simulate the situation where a mask becomes dislodged underwater.

● Moving further from the surface – with the technique mastered the student is then taken into slightly deeper water where they can no longer immediately stand up to regain the surface. This reassures them that the technique works equally well irrespective of depth.

● Consolidation – for such a fundamental skill completing the exercise only once is not really enough. To ensure that the student can perform the skill reliably it needs to be practiced on a number of occasions. Repeating the exercise during a number of different training sessions to consolidate the skill is also a part of the progression.

A complex skill

Some activities are actually composites of a number of different skills and require specific knowledge. An example of such an activity is the lifting of a submerged object. A typical sequence for teaching this skill would include the following:

● Theoretical knowledge – classroom lessons will be required to ensure that the student fully understands buoyancy and the effect of changing pressure on the volume of air used. Any equipment that the students have not seen before, such as buoyancy bags or snap shackles, will need to be fully explained.

● Dry practice – the students will need a chance to become familiar with handling the equipment before they take it into the water. Any knots necessary to attach snap shackles to lifting bags or to the object to be lifted, will need to be demonstrated and practiced by the students. A dry-run of fully assembling the equipment and then disassembling it again for transport will provide a rehearsal of the exercise to be carried out underwater.

● Shallow, sheltered water – using a relatively small object the instructor can demonstrate the technique for inflating the buoyancy bag and how to judge the amount of air required to do so. Student practice then follows until the students are familiar with the technique.

- Deeper water – using the same equipment, the students are introduced to the effects of the greater pressure reducing the rate of inflation of the bag and the effects of air expansion in the bag on ascent.

- More demanding conditions – initially the exercises need to be carried out in clear water and benign conditions but once the basic techniques have been learnt they can be repeated in less favourable conditions of reduced visibility or greater water movement.

- More complex lifts – the relatively small objects used for the initial practices can be replaced with much heavier objects which will require larger lifting bags, more complex attachment arrangements and will have inherently more inertia.

Types of progression

The above examples illustrate a number of different types of progression, each determined by the particular requirements appropriate to the step being taught. These include:

- Sequential build up of the skill – e.g. partial mask flood/full flood/mask removal. This type of progression is the most common where a specific individual skill is being taught.

- Repeating a skill under less benign conditions – e.g. mask clearing at increased depth. Carrying out exactly the same skill but under a different and more demanding set of conditions or with different equipment configurations is no less a progression. The dry-run is an example of one extreme of this progression.

- Sequencing of theory and practical lessons – e.g. understanding what buoyancy is before trying to use it in practice.

The component elements of complex activities need not always follow a specific sequence. Activities such as dive marshalling, for instance, comprise a number of elements, some of which are not directly dependant upon one another and hence need not be learnt in a set sequence e.g. site selection, dive logs. Other activities may comprise elements which, while they may ultimately need to be combined in a specific sequence, can be taught individually in a different sequence e.g. the elements of a complete rescue such as controlled buoyant lift, artificial ventilation, towing, equipment removal, casualty removal from the water. For such activities the progression is achieved by teaching each element individually. Once the elements can be performed to the required standard individually they are then combined.

Personal improvement

Scuba diving is constantly changing with the evolution of new equipment, techniques and our general knowledge of the effects of the diving environment on the human body.

If an instructor fails to remain abreast of these changes it is inevitable that the instructors effectiveness will steadily decline to the detriment of their students.

Figure 110 Demonstrating the deployment of a 'Delayed' Surface Marker Buoy.

Figure 111 Mask clearing at greater depth.

Even if an instructor is able to keep abreast of these changes no one can possibly know everything that there is to know about instructional techniques. By constantly learning about different techniques good instructors will find alternatives that enable them to further improve their effectiveness. What, therefore, are the methods available to instructors which will allow them to continually update their knowledge and skills?.

Instructor qualifications

The most structured avenue for improvement for the newly qualified instructor is to continue the process of gaining further, higher grade, formal instructor qualifications. This is achieved via a series of specific instructor training courses and assessments. The training courses provide the opportunity to learn new techniques and how best to apply known techniques to different situations, while at the same time providing an opportunity for feedback on instructional performance from the course staff. The instructors who staff such events are all chosen for their wide range of instructional experience and their high standards of performance. This ensures that they can provide the best possible tuition in instructional techniques for all stages of diver training. Inducting instructors onto the staff of such events ensures that assessments made and feedback provided are based on a consistent set of standards.

By their very nature, however, such events occur at one point in time. Other mechanisms are needed which enable the instructor to develop skills on a continual basis both to ensure that they remain up-to-date and to further broaden their existing skills.

Keeping up-to-date

Theoretical knowledge
The standard references for the diving instructor are the various diving manuals and it is clearly important that the most up-to-date versions are used. Continued use of old versions of the manuals will not ensure that the instructors theoretical knowledge is updated and will also cause confusion for the students when the instructor teaches information which is at variance with the students' own current version of the manual. Such a situation can only result in a loss of credibility for the instructor.

Reading around the subject of diving as much as possible ensures a broader knowledge base with more indepth knowledge of particular subjects available from specialist manuals. The greater an instructor's understanding of any particular topic, the more confident they will be in teaching it and the more effective the instruction will be.

While manuals and other texts are updated from time to time this is generally a long term process. Diving magazines and periodicals can quickly react to any new developments and are a ready source of information for the diving instructor. Because of their nature, however, magazines will not provide the depth of information that will become available in subsequent manual updates.

Practical skills
Practical skills and techniques evolve as a result of both improvements in our understanding of the diving environment (eg. ascent profiles due to advances in the understanding of decompression requirements) and as a result of developments in equipment (eg. alternate air sources). Many of these advances are covered in diving magazines and manuals and are of such a nature that the instructor can update their own skills with adequate practice. Where the implications of the changes are more substantial (eg. oxygen administration, nitrox diving) specific courses are developed to provide a safe and effective means of disseminating the skills. Attendance on such courses will not only enable the instructor to develop these skills, but also to see the relevant instructional techniques.

Developing instructional techniques

Keeping up-to-date is only one aspect of personal improvement. Attention also needs to be directed towards the instructional techniques used. In this respect a most useful personal attribute is an open mind, not just to be receptive to constructive criticism of personal teaching performance, but to be ready to consider alternative teaching techniques. Frequently there is no one 'right' or 'wrong' technique but a number of alternatives. By learning different techniques the instructor will be more able to adapt their own technique when circumstances demand it, such as when a student is having particular difficulty with an aspect of training.

Just as reading around the subject will help to develop the instructors theoretical knowledge, many ideas for instructional techniques can be gleaned from reading instructional materials from other organisations. Although materials from other diving or water user organisations will provide the most directly applicable ideas, many ideas can be gained from a study of other organisations training materials, as often the techniques can be applied across a range of subjects.

Without some form of feedback it is difficult for an instructor to judge their own personal teaching performance with the obvious possibility of deterioration. Some feedback can be gained by monitoring how readily the student assimilate the knowledge or skills. If they are clearly having difficulties, then a judgement has to be made as to whether this is a problem with the student or with the instruction. The instructor needs to be very honest with themselves if this judgement is to provide a meaningful assessment of the situation. Where a number of students are having the same difficulty, the solution to the problem may lie with the instructor's technique.

With all the will in the World, however, there is a limit to the feedback that can be obtained from self-assessment and an independent view will be far more productive. In this respect instructors within a club or School can assist one another with constructive criticism of each other's performance. It has to be stressed that the criticism needs to be constructive as it is very easy to be destructive and negative. This helps no-one.

Constructive criticism on the other hand not only helps the instructor being monitored, but also develops the thought processes of the instructor doing the monitoring, which they can then reflect into their assessment of their own performance.

This process can therefore be of mutual benefit with the subsequent debrief generating additional ideas which both instructors can use to their advantage.

Within the closed community of a particular club or School there will be a limit to the scope for development, which can only be broadened by the injection of fresh ideas from an external source. The involvement of a wider community of instructors, and hence exposure to a wider variety of instructional techniques, will provide a basis for broadening their scope. This requires the instructor's involvement in activities outside their normal environment.

The most immediate avenue for such involvement is often a reciprocal arrangement with another local club or School. This provides a larger pool of expertise and ideas which can be accessed for the benefit of all the instructors concerned. A further benefit to such an arrangement is to provide additional instructors at times of peak demand.

A more extensive, and in many respects more structured avenue for development, is in becoming involved in Coaching Scheme activities. This not only has the advantage of providing access to a far wider spectrum of expertise, but also provides this access in a very structured manner. Instructional events run at such a level, are required to be run to a consistent national set of standards and consequently instructors are inducted onto such events through a controlled procedure. This induction provides feedback from instructors with a wide range of experience and expertise at a national level with constant monitoring of performance on each event to preserve the standards.

Practical skills

An instructor's practical skills are an essential ingredient of their overall instructional ability. These skills therefore need to be well practiced and up-to-date. The importance of this is relevant not only to those times when an instructor is specifically teaching a lesson but in everything that an instructor does due to the example that they are expected to set.

The importance of a good example

When a student first learns to scuba dive their instructor is often the first diver with whom they have had any real contact. The example that is set will therefore have a significant effect on how that student subsequently behaves as a diver. If the instructor acts in a lackadaisical manner, then it will not be surprising that the student approaches diving in the same manner. Not only will this cause training to take more time than necessary, but there is also an inherent danger. While the instructor has the experience to know which aspects of diving are safety critical, the student does not and hence may not take critical aspects seriously enough with the consequent prejudice to safety.

Even when they are not specifically training, instructors will still be looked upon by less experienced divers as an example to follow. If, for instance, the instructor's equipment is poorly treated and maintained then this will be interpreted as a satisfactory standard. An instructor's bad habits are thus, by default, passed on to the lesser experienced.

Instructors must accept that they are always 'on parade', not just when teaching a specific lesson, and should ensure that their example is worthy of being followed.

Setting high standards

The standard of an instructor's personal skills is important for a number of reasons:

● Unless the instructor can perform a skill himself he will not be able to teach it.

● The standard to which the instructor performs a skill will set the goal to which the students will aspire. Setting the highest standard possible will ensure that the students also strive to achieve a high standard. As it is unlikely that the students will aspire to a higher standard than that set by their instructor, setting a low standard ensures that the students will also achieve a low standard with at least a detrimental effect to their training progress and possible prejudice to their diving safety.

● An instructor who consistently performs to a high standard will gain the respect of the students. This will result in more attention to the tuition on their part and the desire to also achieve high standards, with the consequent benefits to their training and enjoyment of their scuba diving. An instructor who consistently performs to a low standard will quickly lose credibility and the students' respect.

● If an instructor's performance is such that it is clear to the students that the instructor is having some difficulty with the skill, then they will naturally assume that it will be even more difficult for them. A negative expectation will thus have been set which can only be detrimental to the students' own performance.

Maintaining high standards

Any skill that is not frequently exercised will inevitably deteriorate. This is true of both an instructor's personal skills and also their instructional skills. It is important, therefore, that instructors keep in regular practice for all the skills that they may be called upon to teach. Certain skills, which relate to diving safety, should in any case be regularly practiced purely from the viewpoint of the instructor's own diving safety.

Personal Skills

The more basic diving skills are those that are used on every dive and those that the instructor will most commonly be required to teach. Maintaining currency for these skills is not usually a problem, unless for some reason the instructor has had a lay-off from diving. This could be due to illness or just the lower frequency of diving usually experienced during certain seasons. If this occurs, then it is in the instructor's interest to do some refresher practice before instructing any students. Failure to do so could result in embarrassment in front of the students and an inevitable loss of credibility.

Some skills, however, are not used very often. These are generally those of a more specialist nature such as searches, lifting techniques or the use of particular types of navigational equipment. In these cases it is essential that in preparing for the lesson the instructor has carried out recent practice of the skills required. Trying to teach a skill which the instructor has not recently performed is one of the most common causes of poor instructional performance.

Ensuring a good standard of personal skills will therefore benefit the instructor from both a diving and instructional viewpoint. Taking such refresher training seriously will, also set an example for other divers to follow; particularly those who have not undertaken any training for some time and who may therefore be in need of a refresher of some of the more basic skills which they have not exercised recently. Promoting such refresher training by example can only have benefits to overall diving safety and enjoyment of other divers.

New Techniques

Where new developments evolve it is essential that instructors are fully conversant with and capable of performing any new techniques. This involves at least practicing the new techniques to ensure that they can be performed to a high standard. Depending upon the complexity of the actual techniques concerned this may require attendance on a Skill Development Course which will automatically provide the necessary practical instruction.

Instructional Skills

The opportunities for improvement of instructional skills have been addressed elsewhere but, just like any other skill, an instructor's current teaching skills will deteriorate if not exercised. The need for refresher practice of less frequently used personal skills has been discussed above and advantage can be taken of this practice to include instructional aspects.

As the refresher practice progresses the standard to which the skills are performed will improve. Once the skill can be performed comfortably to a high standard, thought can then be given as to how it may be taught. The practice thus effectively migrates into a practice lesson without students. This may entail breaking the skill down into its individual components, each being practiced individually or in sequence until the instructional elements are also performed comfortably to a high standard. It may involve over-emphasizing particular aspects of the skill or performing the skill at a very slow pace.

For underwater lessons, appropriate signals can be included and practiced to ensure that they are naturally clear and more deliberately emphasized. For surface skills, such as boat handling, the development of a running commentary of the actions being taken and the reasons for them can be included.

This instructional refresher practice will be more effective if carried out in conjunction with another instructor. This will not only allow the constructive criticism discussed in the earlier section on *Personal Improvement*, but will enable feedback on such aspects as the instructor's positioning relative to the students. Being able to perform a skill to a high standard is not enough in the instructional context if the students position prevents them from seeing the critical aspects.

The confidence factor

Maintaining a high standard of personal skills will enable an instructor to approach a lesson with confidence and to concentrate on teaching the skills concerned. This will result in higher quality instruction with the resultant high level of student motivation and performance. Not only will the students derive more enjoyment from their training, but this in turn will result in more enjoyment and satisfaction for the instructor.

An instructor with a low standard of personal skills will not achieve the same level of confidence or instructional performance and consequently neither they nor their students will obtain the same enjoyment.

Figure 112 Instructor improving his personal performance.

Assessing Performance

Assessing Performance

As with all sports which carry an element of risk, the quality and effectiveness of the training given are vital. This is important not just for their own well being, but also for the safety of those who will dive with them.

During and on completion of training students are assessed on their proficiency in the practical skills of diving, and on their understanding of the essential theoretical aspects of their chosen sport.

While theory information and practical teaching could be presented without any attempt to see if the student was learning, it would be wasteful and ineffective instruction. If the student failed to understand any basic topic, how could they develop competence in the more complex and demanding aspects? There must be a process for measuring performance at regular intervals throughout a training programme so that the student who is not learning can be identified and given corrective instruction before bad or dangerous habits become too firmly established.

Throughout this manual it has been stressed that poor instruction comes from poor instructors, and the process of lesson analysis not only reveals weaknesses in the students' ability but also in your performance as an instructor. This section deals with how lesson analysis should be applied and tests conducted to measure overall competence during and on completion of training.

Lesson analysis

Use lesson analysis to ensure that your students are learning. The following are suggested methods which you can use to check that your instruction is effective.

During and after each lesson ask yourself the following questions:

● **Are my students learning?**
● **Do my students understand?**
● **Are they performing the skill correctly?**
● **Will it be relevant?**

If the answer is no, there is little point in progressing with more teaching until the things which are not understood are retaught successfully. Fortunately, it is extremely rare to find that nothing has been taught. More common are simple misunderstandings of technique, concept or knowledge, because the demonstration or explanation was not clear enough or defective; or because errors went uncorrected. Since good teaching depends largely on the teaching of essentials, any misunderstanding indicates a weak foundation for future learning on the subject, or poor technique which may not be able to match up to an emergency.

How lessons are analysed

If you are reading this Manual section by section, you will already have a fair idea of how lesson analysis is applied.

The process is most effective in the teaching of practical skills, where progress in simple skill learning is usu-

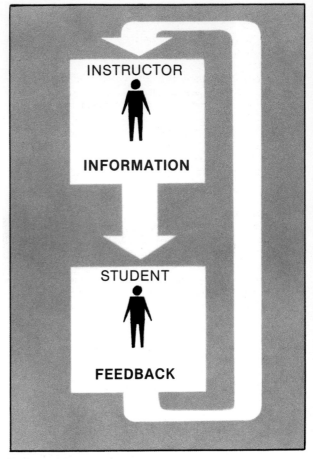

Figure 113 Use feedback to check students are learning.

ally rapid. It can also be applied to complex skills – so long as they have been broken down into a logical series of simple steps (sub-skills) through the process of planned progressive instruction. The programmed teaching approach must be applied consistently to all practical lessons if it is to be of any value.

It can also be used during theory training, but you may have to wait until the end of the lesson to do so. This depends on whether you are prepared to have your students interrupt you to ask questions or seek clarification at any time during the lesson. If you are – or if you pose questions regularly – then the principle is being used.

Another way to check the level of students' knowledge is with a quiz or short test at the end of the theory lesson. If the results indicate some significant gaps in their knowledge then parts of the lesson may have to be repeated using a different teaching approach. Always plan your lessons to include opportunities to measure whether students are learning.

Continuous assessment

It could be argued that, if programmed teaching is applied to every lesson, then each one will include some form of test or evaluation.

Only if each lesson objective or skill is achieved does the student progress to the next lesson. This is the principle of continuous assessment.

In some situations, this type of evaluation process replaces final tests. It works well for practical skills assessments, but less well for theory training, unless regular short tests are made following each classroom lesson. As an assessment skill, you should be aware of it, but it has no place in current teaching methods for BSAC diver training.

Theory tests and examinations

In addition to completing practical tests during training, it is usual to assess a students' knowledge of essential theory by conducting a theory test before diving qualifications are awarded. It is important that this test checks the correct things – what the student needs to know to dive safely, and to look after themselves and their buddy. A theory test should not only check that knowledge is retained, but that it can also be properly applied.

Tests can be conducted by oral questions or by written examinations. The merits of each method will be considered in this section, as well as the duration of theory tests, their marking, and the different questioning techniques.

Figure 114 Students sitting a written exam.

What to ask

This manual puts a great deal of emphasis on defining objectives, and teaching students what they need to know in order to achieve them. If the emphasis in theory training is on essential information, it will be obvious that a theory test can only ask questions on the same area of knowledge. This is very much the case when the qualification is a basic one, such as a beginner in a swimming pool. All theory test questions should be carefully prepared so that they check whether the student has learnt, and knows how to apply, the essential information.

The student will have acquired a lot of facts as a result of training and should have a fair idea of how to apply them. However, they are unlikely to have sufficient knowledge to develop and express opinions on subjects, therefore it is better to stick to assessing factual and practical knowledge and avoid questions where the answer is a matter of opinion.

Where the theory test is for a more advanced student, such as a diver with open water experience, a wider knowledge should be expected and a test can include some non essential knowledge and can invite comments. For advanced examinations, the ideal question may ask the student to bring two or three principles together and then apply them to a problem.

An advanced theory test can also look back on previous training and check that earlier items are still remembered and understood. Where subjects are not repeated or developed during training for higher qualifications, the theory test may be the only opportunity to find out if the student can still remember and apply knowledge learnt during basic training.

Written or oral?

Once you have decided on the scope of the test, you need to decide whether the test will be written or oral. This decision will have a bearing on the way the questions are worded or posed.

Written examinations can use a greater variety of questioning techniques (e.g. multiple choice, matching questions, essays) whereas an oral test will involve fairly short questions, and expect equally brief answers.

If necessary, oral questions can be given to supplement a written test, or to clarify written answers where it is thought that the question may have been misleading or misunderstood. For higher diving qualifications, general knowledge can be checked by a written test, and opinions by oral questioning.

The advantages and disadvantages of each type of test:

Written theory tests

- A large number of students can take the test at the same time.

- All students answer the same questions, so the standard is uniform and fair.

- Can be conducted by any reliable invigilator – diving knowledge unnecessary.

- Students may suffer from 'exam nerves' or have difficulty in compiling written answers (an oral test would be better for them).

- Does not permit supplementary questioning to clarify answers, hence the wording of questions must be clear and unambiguous.

Oral theory tests

- Ideal for a single student.

- An oral test can often be more relaxed and informal. The examiner can put the student at ease.

- Questions can be rephrased if the student does not understand them, and some prompting is possible if necessary.

- It is possible to announce a clear pass immediately after the test.

- Requires the presence of an experienced instructor to conduct and invigilate the exam.

- It takes a long time to conduct individual oral tests for a large number of students

- A good selection of questions is necessary – one student is sure to pass the gist of questions on to another student.

- Not very suitable where reasoned opinion answers need to be developed – this can be done better as a written essay answer.

- Unsuitable if large numbers need to be tested.

Compiling questions

Theory test questions should be compiled from the lesson notes prepared by the instructor for each specific topic. In this way, questions are based on the material taught, and not what the instructor thinks may have been taught. Other questions can be taken from the appropriate textbooks which are required reading for the student during training.

When you work with a team of fellow instructors on the same training programme, the process of compiling examination questions can be speeded up if all are involved. Another way of making the task simpler, is to either draw questions from, or model them on, those in the publications issued by the respective scuba diver training agency.

Plan to ask at least three questions within each important subject area. Questions should be devised to determine a students' appreciation of safety and good diving practice.

It is good practice to compile and hold a number of questions and answers which are suitable for either written or oral presentation – or which can be quickly modified to make them suitable. It can save a great deal of time and effort when a test paper is needed in a hurry. The questions can also be used during lessons to check whether students are learning (programmed teaching).

It is essential that questions and theory tests are compiled and conducted with care. This will ensure a uniform standard and reduces ambiguities in questions.

Compile your lists of questions and answers at the same time, to ensure that your answers are drawn from the same source as the questions. The pass standard should be established and a marking scheme devised. If necessary, allocate notional marks to each question.

Wording of questions

Questions should be carefully worded so that the meaning is quite clear to the student and so that only one answer – the correct one – is likely to result. Consider other interpretations of your phrasing – if you do not, be assured the student will! Any questions with vague and ambiguous wording will result in vague answers. Such questions do not represent a realistic means of assessing a students' knowledge.

Ask another member of your instructor team to check through the list of questions and answers to avoid ambiguity. Questions which seek opinions are the most difficult to evaluate, but these normally only occur when higher qualifications are being assessed.

Correct and unambiguous wording is important as the following examples illustrate.

Question: What would be your action as a Dive Marshal if a scuba diver has made an emergency ascent?
The word *would* has been used instead of *should*.
The question asks for a reaction -shout .... scream ...... rush about – rather than what ought to happen. The question also suffers form a lack of detail i.e. from what depth was the emergency ascent made? .... What caused the emergency?, etc.

Question: Write down the main points to be stressed when teaching Artificial Ventilation.

This assumes that everyone taking the test intends to become an instructor. Even instructors are not expected to memorise the contents of all lessons, therefore ensure that questions are relevant to the qualification standard.

Question: Draw the symbol that would be used on an Admiralty Chart for the following features......

It is reasonable for divers to understand charts, but not to be able to draw them. By all means ask for symbols to be identified to ascertain knowledge on the subject.

Duration of theory tests

This depends mainly on the diving grade to which the test applies. The more advanced the qualification, the longer and more searching the examination will be. The wording of the questions and the speed at which they can be answered play a very important part in deciding how long a test takes. The duration should be based on the number of questions to be answered, rather than on a set time limit, although a time limit is usually imposed in most externally assessed examinations.

Conduct of theory tests

Students should only attempt a test when the instructor considers them ready. Some students may require some encouragement to take the test, however failure of the test for which a student is unprepared will be a blow to their motivation. At the same time, if a student is eager and ready for the test, an unnecessary delay can also diminish their interest and motivation.

Figure 115 Oral exams are useful for individual students.

Figure 116 Students under practical examination.

Announce the date, time and venue for the theory test well in advance, this gives time for final study and preparation.

Oral Tests: Choose a quiet, comfortable venue. Put the student at ease and advise them of the ground rules for the test i.e. you will only accept their first answer, you will not discuss the answers until the end of the test etc.

Ask questions clearly and repeat them if necessary. If you need to make notes, try not to distract the student by doing so. After the examination you may comment on the answers if you wish.

If a student has to make a calculation during an oral exam, the necessary materials should be supplied. Have pens, pencils, paper to hand for this purpose. Calculators are often allowed where the student is required to work out answers which require numerical results.

Written Tests: Choose a venue with sufficient light, table space and chairs. Reduce outside distractions to a minimum. When the students are seated, check that everyone has the materials required, pens, paper etc. Give them any special instructions. Distribute the examination papers, usually face-down. Start all the students at the same time and let them know the time limit for the test.

Let the students know when they have reached the half-way stage and also when there is only a short time remaining. Stop everyone writing at the same time and collect up all the papers before the students disperse.

Figure 117 Using an underwater slate is useful when assessing a practical performance.

Assessment of results

Results of theory tests should be measured against the standards established for the test and diving qualification objectives. Once they are set, care must be taken to ensure they are maintained. There should be no variation from the laid down standards. Usually theory tests – oral or written – are assessed by more than one person, ideally those who compiled the questions and set the standards. The pass standard should be agreed in advance. Since the majority of questions will be testing essential information, a pass mark above 50% should be looked for in order to maintain an acceptable standard.

It is also important that the examination results reveal no blank areas in the students' knowledge. It may be possible for a student to achieve a pass mark and yet fail to answer correctly any of the questions in an important subject area. Students should be expected to attain a pass mark in all groups of questions covering important subject areas within the scuba diver training programme.

When assessing results, clear passes or failures are easily identified. Borderline cases may require more careful analysis. If the student would have passed with more time, because they happen to be a slow reader or writer, perhaps extra time should be given or supplementary oral questions asked in order to see which way the balance tips.

Failures should be looked at closely to determine whether the lack of knowledge is 'across the board' or specific to any subject. If the former, perhaps they were not ready for the test. If the latter, have they missed theory sessions, or just not understood? Bad test results do not just reflect on the student, they can also indicate poor instruction, with failure to check that learning is taking place (programmed teaching), or a badly-prepared examination paper. A high number of failures among students taking the same written paper could be an indication of poorly constructed questions.

Where questions invite opinion or are of essay type, you should take extra care to mark them objectively, rather than allowing your own opinion to over-ride your judgement.

Announcing results

Students will be anxious to know how they have fared in the test, so results should be announced as soon as possible following the event. Long delays suggest bad news and this can affect your students' motivation. It is best to publish and display a list of passes.

This gives a little boost to those who have passed, and it will be obvious to those who have failed that their names are omitted from the list. Individual marks should not be included in the published list. Clearly, students who have failed should be notified beforehand and in private so that they can receive further guidance for study and assistance. Provide an early opportunity for the failures to re-take the test and give additional coaching to help them to pass next time.

Practical tests

It is important that instructors teach students what they need to know, not how to pass tests. Tests present no difficulty to students who are correctly trained. This could mean that those who do have difficulty then taking final tests, may not have been thoroughly trained. Remember it is good training that matters, not tests.

If the process of programmed teaching is followed a student will be continually assessed during training. It can be argued that continuous assessment should replace tests, but the one thing that tests do is see that the student can 'get it all together', when under some degree of stress.

Contents of practical tests

Practical tests should examine the student on all the skills they need to know for that particular level of diving qualification. Therefore, for higher grades, it is reasonable to include a check on basic abilities as well. The simplest way to conduct practical tests is to ask the student to perform an essential skill in a natural or logical sequence, which could be published as a test schedule or programme.

In the case of tests relating to scuba diving proficiency it is a good idea to conduct them as dives (in swimming pool or open water) during which certain skills/techniques should be demonstrated.

Buddy pairs can work together in lifesaving or buddy breathing situations. It is unlikely that the instructor would be involved in the test – as a rescue victim, because to do so would place the instructor in a position where they could not accurately assess all aspects of the students' performance of the skill.

Preparation of tests

Students should take tests when all relevant training has been completed and when the instructor is confident that they will pass. Remember that success will maintain motivation, whereas failure could dampen it. Failure in tests must also bring into question the ability and thoroughness of the instruction. Do not be tempted to put your students forward for tests unless they are truly ready.

Students must be given advance notice of the test so that they can prepare themselves mentally and physically. They should understand beforehand what the test contains, and the sequence in which it is to be carried out. A detailed briefing should precede the test and all equipment being used should be adequate for the purpose. There is some merit in asking a fellow instructor to conduct the test if you have trained the students.

A poor performance can sometimes be allowed if the students' performance during earlier training was acceptable, and if it is considered that a touch of exam nerves has temporarily affected their performance.

When assessing test performance, you must have clearly in your mind the aims and training objectives which the students are attempting to reach. Is the student performing with a level of skill applicable to the aim? If so, they should pass the test. If not, they should fail. Do avoid the common fault of slowly, almost unknowingly raising the standard.

Positioning

The examining instructor should occupy the best vantage point to observe the test. The poolside side for surface activities: underwater with the students to observe scuba skills. The same applies to open water tests: on the surface or underwater, whichever gives you the best viewpoint from which to assess performance.

'Value analysis' of tests

The examiner should also consider the value of various parts of a performance. Some skills are more valuable than others in terms of safety – the essential skills – and a good performance in them should tip the balance in favour of the student who might be weak on some less important part of the test schedule.

Judge the overall performance, not specific aspects of the test. Tell students of any weaknesses in the debriefing. The motivation boost they will receive by passing will ensure their determination to overcome their faults, and they can do this through practice and experience.

Figure 118 Occupy the best vantage point during assessment.

BSAC Instructor Grades

Becoming a BSAC instructor

In many instances, diving accidents are found to be the result of poor diving practice, and this is often the result of ineffective instruction. Ineffective instruction usually comes from poor quality instructors!

It is essential that every scuba instructor is trained to instruct in the most effective way. The skills required usually include classroom teaching, teaching initial skills in "sheltered water" or a swimming pool, teaching scuba skills from a shore and/or a boat, teaching aspects of seamanship etc.

The following Instructor Training Scheme has been developed over many years by the BSAC and is continuously monitored and adjusted to keep pace with the changes in sport diving techniques and equipment.

Assistant Instructor

To gain an insight into the art of teaching you can attend a 2 day BSAC Instructor Training Course (ITC) once you have reached the level of Sports Diver.

Attendance at this event is the first step in the learning process, where you are shown how to teach in the most effective way in the classroom and in the swimming pool.

Club Instructor

When you have reached the Dive Leader standard, you can attend a 1 day Club Instructor Examination (CIE) where your ability to teach in the classroom and in the swimming pool are tested, along with a test of your theoretical knowledge. If you meet the required standard on the examination, you are awarded the qualification of BSAC Club Instructor. Club Instructor is the first nationally awarded grade of instructor.

Open Water Instructor Course

The Open Water Instructor course is a 1 day course and is intended to provide BSAC Club Instructors with the skills and knowledge required to teach techniques in the open water environment.

Instructors can obtain the qualification of Open Water Instructor after completing twelve hours of logged instructional experience after attending the course. The course consists of a presentation on open water teaching techniques and a group planning session of open water lessons followed by several practical sessions where Course Instructors demonstrate various teaching skills which are then practiced by the students.

Advanced Instructor

The next grade of instructor is open to divers who have reached the Advanced Diver standard, and who are already Club Instructors and Open Water Instructors.

You can attend a 2 day Advanced Instructor Course (AIC) where you will be shown how to maximize the teaching opportunities when teaching in the classroom, teaching scuba skills from the shore, teaching scuba and seamanship skills in and from a small boat. When you feel ready to be examined at this level you can apply to take a theoretical examination before the attending the practical examination. If successful, you can then attend a 2 day Advanced Instructor Examination (AIE) where your teaching skills in the classroom, from the shore and from a boat are assessed.

If successful, you will be awarded the BSAC Advanced Instructor qualification.

National Instructor

If your ambition is to reach the highest level, and become someone who is an expert at teaching other Instructors and running any of the BSAC courses or exams – the BSAC National Instructor Award is the top instructional award of the BSAC. Having already qualified as an Advanced Instructor you must first become a BSAC First Class Diver. This involves a 3-hour theory paper and a 2 day practical examination. If successful you can then sit a 1 hour theory paper on instructional matters and, attend a 4 day practical examination where ALL aspects of diving and instruction are assessed. Those successful in the event will be awarded the BSAC National Instructor qualification.

National Instructors are the people the BSAC rely on to organizeand control its Instructor Training Scheme and Skill Development Courses. A number of National Instructors could be regarded as "International" Instructors since the BSAC enlists their talents to run courses and exams for the many overseas BSAC Branches and BSAC Schools.

Other diver training agencies have similar, though different, Instructor training systems. There is a "crossover" system which allows instructors from other agencies to convert and become qualified instructors in the BSAC.

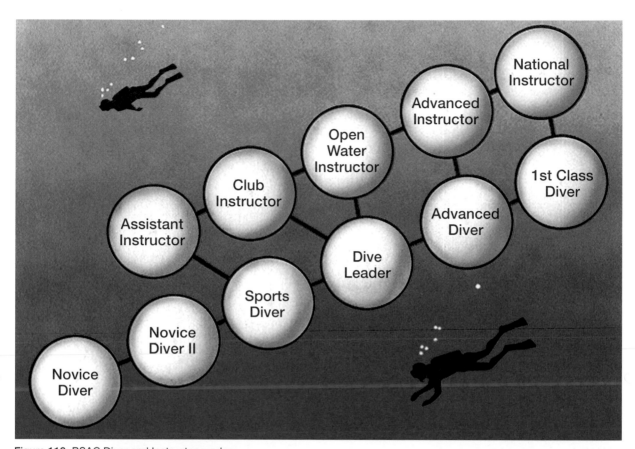

Figure 119 BSAC Diver and Instructor grades

Figure 120 BSAC Instructor Badges

Index

Illustrations can be found on the pages shown in italics

Illustration Acknowledgements

Thanks are due to the following for allowing the use of copyright photographs:

Mike Busuttili, figures 1, 4-6, 34-35, 45, 62-63, 65, 71-72, 74, 76, 83-85, 88, 91-93, 95-97, 99-106, 109-112, 116-118;
Diver Magazine, figures 31, 40-42;
Jerry Hazzard, figures 43-44;
Mike Holbrook, figures 13, 20, 49, 64, 114;
Hugh Jackson, figures 2-3, 17, 21-24, 27-30, 32, 36, 37-38, 46-48, 51, 53-56, 73, 75, 78, 87, 98, 107, 115;
Lucy Powell, figure 120.

Photographs opening each section are by Mike Busuttili (Practical Teaching, Visual Aids, Teaching Basic Skills, Teaching in Open Water, Assessing Performance), Diver Magazine (Advanced Lecturing), Mike Holbrook (The Learning Process), Hugh Jackson (The Scuba Instructor, The Teaching Process, Classroom Teaching).

All the artwork in this manual was specially commissioned from Rico Oldfield.

The British Sub-Aqua Club would like to express its appreciation to Nutec Centre for Safety Limited Billingham and Centre International Plongee Nice for the use of their facilities while taking a number of photographs for this manual.